# Influence Human Behavior

-

## Understanding Cognitive Behavioral Therapy and True NLP Science to Improve Yourself and Influence People around You

Table of Contents

Introduction

What does it mean to influence human behavior?
Influence is a process in social psychology during which
changes in an individual's behavior, feelings, emotions, or
opinions that occur due to what other people do for him,
including as a result of targeted influence and manipulation.
Social influence can take different forms and can be taken
within the framework of a social contract, can take the form of
pressure, be the occasion and the result of obedience,
leadership, persuasion, and also the result of marketing.

Types of influence
In 1958, a psychologist at Harvard University, Herbert
Kelman, identified and described three main types of
influence:

- conformism - the individual, it would seem, agrees with
  the opinions of others, but in reality retains his opinion;
- identification - the individual is influenced by authority;
- internalization ( acceptance ) - people accept
  convictions imposed by influence and agree with them,
  both outside and inside.

Morton Deutsch and Harold Gerard describe two
psychological needs that lead a person to adapt to the
expectations of others. This is the need to maintain a positive
self-image of informational social influence and the need to be
socially acceptable (normative social influence ).

Informational influence is influence in order to receive
transmitted information from someone as a fact describing
reality. Information impact takes place in a situation where the
recipient's opinion is uncertain. In the context of the Kelman
typology, informational influence leads to the conformity of
the individual with society and the acceptance of the facts of
social reality.

Chapter 1
Pride and influence: how to learn to manage people
Knowledge of human psychology and the basics of how to
manage people is necessary not only for a leader or a
businessman. Such knowledge will be useful to any person for
building a career, creating successful personal relationships,
mutually beneficial interaction with people around them. They
will be useful in the family, when communicating with
relatives, friends, neighbors.

Some very capable individuals from nature have management
skills. They intuitively feel how psychologically to influence
other people, to earn their authority, to incline to their
opinion, to push them to certain actions and actions.

Even in the children's sandbox there is always a leader.

But even if by nature you are not a craftsman to manage
everyone in the yard and not the most powerful guy in the
village, the ability to influence other people can still be
developed by studying and applying numerous techniques and
methods of influencing others.

1.1 Human psychology: how to manage people
When you want to expand the boundaries of your capabilities,
achieve a certain material level and high prestige in society,
then you have no choice but to learn how to influence people.
Your goal is to establish contact with others, to earn trust, to
become an authority, to motivate you to perform certain
actions that are beneficial to you, using the emotional and
psychological component of the personality. How to
psychologically influence people, trying to achieve certain
goals? The following proven methods of action will help.

Use arguments
An important step towards knowing how to learn how to
manage people is the selection of the right argument. All
requests, requests and wishes are always supported by
convincing arguments. Your requirements should be

immaculate in terms of necessity and expediency. Even the most unusual and difficult tasks will be solved with great enthusiasm, if they have a logical basis.

## Dose important information

If you are a carrier of information that has a certain value for any circle of people, then learn how to properly present it. This should be convincing, confident, but very quickly and in small quantities. Leave an intrigue, understatement, make others think, worry, feel responsibility. Influencing other people, using information, is easy - provide it in small portions. Over time, all your words will find meaning and will be perceived as something that cannot be doubted.

## Potential danger

You do not know how to influence people's behavior, then use their fears . And not necessarily real. Such a danger can be unobtrusively suggestible and developed, based on even the insignificant facts provided by themselves. To win the trust of a person, win over to your side, bind to yourself, and offer yourself support and help in a difficult situation. By participating in solving a problem, you form a strong dependency. A person will be grateful, he will consider himself due. Of course, after that he will not refuse your request and will help with all his might.

## Right choice

How to influence the behavior of people so that they do what you need, without visible coercion. Give them the opportunity to choose from several possible solutions. Freedom of choice is a good incentive for a person who encourages being active and productive. You will achieve it if others believe that they choose independently, although in reality only one result is possible in the situation - the one you need.

## Cohesion

Get close to the people you want to control. Combine and unite a team or family with a common idea. Use the image of an enemy who threatens the well-being, health, safety or market position. Fear of a common threat brings together, strengthens relations in a team and forms a strong interdependence. It makes you mobilize, act more efficiently and more productively to achieve the aforementioned common goal and is one of the effective ways to psychologically influence people. Your task in such a situation is to only correctly guide people.

1.2 How to learn to manage people? Strive for mutual benefit! In the field of human psychology, the question of how to manage people is one of the most popular. It is important to comply with the measure, without slipping into obvious manipulation. If you use others only to achieve your goals, then such tactics will eventually fail. Most people sooner or later expose your true motivation, and the reaction to it will be resentment, hostility, anger, disgust and even revenge.

Before looking for effective ways to influence other people, consider whether they lead to mutually beneficial interaction. While pursuing your interests, do not forget that the second side must also receive something useful, valuable in return. Only mutually beneficial cooperation between people can be a ground for profit. And only in this case, the actions will be productive and will allow to achieve regular, rather than one-time results. Use the ability to influence people wisely, without creating around them the aura of a manipulator playing with only one goal.

Chapter 2
Principles of persuasion (6 Cialdini's principles)
Few have the good fortune to possess this gift; most of us are deprived of it. How to get a talent of conviction, if the most talented practitioners can not pass it? Turn to science. Over the past fifty years, scientists have discovered some ways in which people can be made to give in, to submit or to change their point of view.

Six Principles of the Science of Persuasion by Robert Cialdini

A handful of naturally gifted people just know how to grab the attention of the audience, win over the indecisive and dissuade the opposition. It captures not only the ease with which they use personal charm and eloquence to convince others to do what they want, but also the zeal with which people perform what is required.

Sadly, these innate masters of the conviction are often not able to realize their wonderful gift or pass it on to others. This complex problem faces the leaders of organizations where every day it is necessary to think out how to motivate and direct the labor force, which has a high level of individualism. The principle "I am the boss, and that says it all" does not work. Even if this principle would not demean and demoralize all interested parties, it would still be out of place in a world where there are cross-functional teams, joint ventures and partnerships of different enterprises, factors blurring the boundaries of power. Under such conditions, the talent of persuasion has a much stronger impact on people's behavior than the formal power structures.

Behavioral scientists have conducted experiments that shed light on some of the techniques that cause people to give in, obey, or change their point of view. A conviction works when it affects a limited set of deep human motives and needs, and it works in a very predictable way. Conviction, in other words, is governed by basic principles that can be taught and which can be studied and applied. Here are the shared ideas of Robert Cialdini.

1. The principle of similarity
Application: find real similarities and offer genuine praise.

If you want to influence people, make them your friends. How? Two factors are especially important here: likeness and praise. In one experiment, described in an article from 1968, published in the Journal of Personality, participants physically stood closer to each other after learning that they had a common view on policy issues and that they shared the same social values. And in 1963, in an article published in the American Behavioral Scientists, researcher F. B. Evans used demographic data from insurance company reports to demonstrate that potential customers were inclined to buy insurance from a vendor who was either about the same age as them, the same religion, or he shared their political opinions, or simply also smoked.

Managers can use affinity to connect with a new employee, head of another department, or even a new boss. Informal conversations during work hours create an ideal opportunity to find at least one common topic. It is important to establish communication early, as this will create grounds for goodwill and trust in subsequent conversations. It is much easier to enlist support for a new project when you have already endeared the people you are trying to convince to take part in this project.

Praise is another reliable method to bind people to yourself, and flatters and disarms. Positive remarks about the features of another person, his attitude to work or about the performance of his work, in turn, create a steady sympathy, as well as a desire to follow what the person who praises him wants. Along with cultivating fruitful relationships, leaders can also use praise to restore spoiled or unproductive relationships.

2. The principle of reciprocity
Application: let's get what you want.

Man obeys the universal tendency to treat people the way they treat him. If you have ever caught yourself smiling at a colleague just because he or she smiled at you first, you know how this principle works.

Charities rely on reciprocity to increase their funds. For years, for example, the Disabled American Veterans Organization used only a well-written letter to collect donations and received only 18% of responses to its appeal. But when this organization began to attach a small gift in an envelope, the response rate almost doubled and reached 35%. The gifts were extremely modest, but the point was not what the intended donors were receiving. The point was that they got something at all.

Gifts are also remarkably long held in memory. I asked readers to send me examples from their own lives, illustrating the principles of influence at work. One reader is an employee from Oregon. She sent a letter in which she cites the following reasons for her attachment to her boss:

"He gives me and my son presents for Christmas and for my birthday. My position does not imply promotion, and the only way to make a career is to move to another department. My boss will soon reach retirement age, and I think I can move to another department after he quits ... But now I feel obliged to stay, since he is so good to me. "

A gift is one of the rougher examples of the rule of reciprocity. More subtle uses of this rule can be expressed as manifestations of trust, a spirit of cooperation, or friendly disposition.

3. The principle of social proof: people follow a similar example of others.
Application: people of equal status convince each other better.

Being essentially social beings, people rely to a large extent on signals from others about how to think, feel and act. These intuitive assumptions have been confirmed in practice. For example, in 1982, the following experiment was described in the Journal of Applied Psychology. A group of researchers walked through apartments in the city of Columbia, (South Carolina) and asked for donations for a charity campaign, showing a list of local residents who had already given money. The researchers found that the longer the list of donators, the more likely it will be made new donations.

For the people who were asked to donate, the names of friends and neighbors on the list were a form of social testimony about how they should act. When there were unfamiliar names on the list, the effect was no longer so strong. In an experiment conducted in the 1960s and described in the Journal of Personality and Social Psychology, New Yorkers were asked to return a lost wallet to its owner. The wallet was returned with great enthusiasm when they learned that another New Yorker had already done the same. But if this other was a foreigner, the enthusiasm was almost gone.

Managers can learn the following lesson from these two experiments: persuasion can be extremely effective when it comes from equals. Imagine that you are trying to modernize the process of your department. A group of old-timers resists. Instead of convincing employees of the advantages of modernization yourself, ask an employee who has been working for a long time and supports your initiative to do this at the general meeting of the department. The speech of a colleague-colleague will have much more chances to convince the group than the next speech of the head. Presented in a simple form, the effect works best horizontally rather than vertically.

4. The principle of consistency
Application: the commitment of people must be made active, public and voluntary.

Having expressed their point of view or taking a certain position, most people prefer to adhere to it. Even a small commitment can powerfully affect future actions. Israeli researchers whose article appeared in the Personality and Social Psychology Bulletin from 1983, they asked half of the residents of a large residential complex to sign a petition in favor of creating a recreation center for the disabled. It was a noble cause, and the request was a small favor, so almost everyone who was interviewed agreed to sign. Two weeks later, on a national day of donations for the disabled, all the residents of the complex were approached and asked to make a donation on the same occasion. Just over half of those who did not sign the petition made a donation. But an amazing amount (92%) of those who signed the petition gave money. Residents of the complex felt obliged to demonstrate their commitment to the project, because their choice was made independently, publicly and voluntarily.

There is vivid empirical evidence that a choice made independently and pronounced out loud, recorded or confirmed in any other incontrovertible way, will more clearly direct further behavior than when the same choice is not confirmed. In 1996, in the journal Personality and Social Psychology Bulletin, Delia Cioffi and Randy Garner described an experiment in which college students were divided into two groups. One group was asked to fill out a form that said that they voluntarily advocate for the introduction of an AIDS education course in public schools. Students from another group were asked to volunteer to speak for the same project, leaving blank a form saying that they would not support the project. A few days later, when volunteers were told about the start of the course, 74% of those who came were students of the group that filled out the forms.

The conclusion is obvious: if a manager wants to convince a subordinate to act in a certain way, he must receive confirmation of this in writing. Suppose you want an employee to submit reports in a timely manner. As soon as you obtain consent from him, ask him to summarize his decision in a memo and send it to you. By doing this, you increase the chances of fulfilling an obligation, because, as a rule, people follow what they themselves wrote.

Desiring to reinforce the commitment of the subject to previously given obligations, confirm these obligations publicly. This can be done by sending an email to the employee saying: "I showed your plan to Diana from the production department and to Phil from the delivery department. They also think the plan is right." No matter how these obligations are formalized, they should by no means resemble the promises that people give themselves on the New Year's Eve and which they then safely forget. They must be made public and articulated clearly.

More than 300 years ago Samuel Butler wrote a couplet, which briefly explains why the commitments to be taken voluntarily to serve for a long time and effectively, "Who will go against the will of his pressure, he still remains at the opinion." If a commitment was made under duress, pressure, or imposed by someone, it has nothing to do with commitment; it is an unpleasant burden.

If you want a fundamental change in a person's behavior to occur, you shouldn't threaten him or put pressure on him to follow his obligations. He can view any change in behavior as a result of intimidation, rather than a personal commitment. The best method is to identify something that a person truly appreciates in work, and then explain to him that your wish is compatible with these values. This will serve as a basis for him to change his behavior. As the person makes these changes on his own, he will continue to control his behavior even when you do not watch him closely.

5. The principle of power
Application: prove that you are a professional; don't think that is self-evident

Two thousand years ago, the Roman poet Virgil gave this simple advice to those who seek to make the right choice: "Trust a knowledgeable person." In the midst of the abundant complexity of modern life, a properly selected expert offers a valuable and effective way to make good decisions. Indeed, some questions - legal, financial, medical or technological - require such profound special knowledge to answer that we have no choice but to rely on the opinion of an expert in this field. Leaders must by all means try to establish themselves as knowledgeable people in their field, and only then try to exert influence.

Surprisingly, people often mistakenly assume that others knowingly recognize and value their experience. That is exactly what happened in the hospital where my colleagues and I were invited. Physiotherapists were upset that many stroke patients stopped performing the necessary exercises as soon as they were discharged from the hospital. No matter how hard the doctors argued that the exercises should be constantly performed at home - and this is actually the only condition for restoring independent functioning - their words did not reach the goal.

Conversations with some of the patients helped to determine the essence of the problem. They knew about the education and work experience of their doctors, but not the physiotherapists, who urged them to continue to work at home. The question was only to fill in the missing information. We simply asked the director of the therapeutic department to hang up all the letters, diplomas and certificates of staff on the walls of the offices. The result was stunning: the number of patients who agreed to do the exercises jumped to 34% and has not decreased since.

Nothing needed to be invented; there was no need to spend either time, or energy, or money on this process. The professionalism of the staff was real: all we had to do was just present it in the right light.

6. The principle of scarcity: people want more of what they
have.
Application: highlight unique advantages and exclusive
information.

Products and capabilities seem more valuable when they
become less accessible. Honestly telling a colleague that you
can miss the last opportunity to talk with the boss before his
departure for a long vacation, you can radically change the
plan of action.

The power of "language loss" was demonstrated in 1988 in a
study among California homeowners, described in the Journal
of Applied Psychology. Half of the homeowners were told that
if they insulate their homes, they will save a certain amount of
money every day. The other half were told that if they did not
warm their houses, they would lose the same amount every
day. Significantly more people insulate their homes with those
who spoke the language of loss. The same thing happens in
business: a potential loss is much more influenced by a
manager's decision than a potential profit.

When making proposals, managers should also remember that
exclusive information is more convincing than widely available
information. My doctoral candidate, Amram Knishinski, in
1982 undertook a study of the decisions of wholesalers to buy
beef. He noted that they more than doubled their orders when
they received information about adverse weather conditions
abroad and possible shortages of foreign beef in the near
future. But their orders increased by 600% when they were
told that no one else had this information.

The next time the exclusive information is in your hands, use it
to strengthen your influence. The information itself may not
be too significant, but exclusivity will give it a special weight.
For example, you can say: "I received this report only today. It
cannot be announced until next week, but I want you to know
about it in advance. " You will see how the interest of your
listeners will increase.

However, remember: you must be sincere. If the deception is detected (and this is sure to happen), any enthusiasm that your words will initially cause will be destroyed.

Two important notes

These six principles of persuasion, without false profundity and mystery, accurately codify our intuitive understanding of information evaluation and decision-making methods. Even people without formal psychological education can easily learn these principles. However, during the seminars and conferences, I became convinced of the need for two things.

Although these six principles and their methods of application for clarity can be discussed separately, they need to be used together to increase the impact. For example, when discussing the importance of professionalism, I suggested that managers use informal social conversations to declare themselves as professional. But these conversations also provide the opportunity not only to transmit information, but also to receive it. Speaking about your skills and experience, you can also learn about your companion's past, preferences and dislikes. Such information will help you identify genuine similarities and sincerely give him compliments. Showing your competence and receiving feedback, you double your power of persuasion.

Standard rules of ethical behavior apply to social influence. The tactics of deception or pressure acts only for a short time. It is detrimental to use these techniques for a long time, especially in organizations that cannot function without a high level of trust and cooperation. This is especially clearly seen in the example that the head of a department of one large textile factory gave during a training seminar conducted by me. She described the vice-president of her company, who believed that she very dexterously forced department heads to publicly commit themselves. Instead of giving his subordinates time to thoroughly discuss and ponder their proposals, he personally came to them in the midst of work and began a long and tedious description of the benefits of his plan, as if experiencing the patience of others. Then he proceeded to a decisive blow. "Your help in this matter is very important to me," he said. "Can I count on your support?" Tired, eager to expel this man from his office, to return to work, the heads of departments always agreed with him. But since the commitments were not accepted voluntarily, the heads of departments never fulfilled them, and as a result, the initiatives of the vice-president collapsed or were forgotten.

This story made a strong impression on the other participants in the seminar. Some were shocked to find out their own manners in the manipulative behavior of the protagonist of this story. Pressure and manipulation when using the principles of social influence are ineffective. However, when properly applied, these principles can lead you to outstanding results.

Chapter 3

## Characteristic traits of persuasive people

Have you ever wondered, what is it that makes some people so persuasive? People with persuasion stand out for their unique talent to be able to persuade those around them about what they believe with arguments. Although they differ quite a bit from each other, people with persuasion share some common features.

### Positivity

The first key feature of people with persuasion is the positive sign of their character. Energy and positive mood will make one more convinced when he has a positive person towards him. But if that does not happen then the chances are few to convince anyone.

### Self confidence

It is important to give confidence to the person you have before you if you really want to convince him of what you say. Confidence is one of the key features of people with persuasion, explaining why they do so well.

### Empathy

Persons persuaded by the concept of empathy, which they have incorporated into their lives, may be able to know the beliefs and needs of other people. So, their work to convince them is much easier.

### They are good listeners

It is very important in a conversation to be able to hear carefully what your interlocutor says. This way you can respond with better arguments to what you are saying. This is a feature that people with persuasion hold very well.

### Willingness to compromise

Sometimes, in order to win the greatest war, you have to concede small battles. This also applies to everyday interpersonal relationships. If you can not reconcile, you will be permanently lost in a conversation. The secret is knowing when to do back to win the next fight. And people with persuasion know very well how to do this.

It is important to know when to get it
He needs attention when you are in a heated debate. The one who first asks, is also the one who loses. Stay silent, listen carefully to your interlocutor and ask when you need to. If you hurry you will have lost a lot of ground. This is a feature that only people with persuasion have.

Authenticity
It sounds strange and yet one of the key features of these people. If you are not authentic in a conversation you risk losing your opponent. Most people with persuasion know that if you do not tell the truth no one is going to trust you.

Flexibility
It is important that you can leave the plan you have prepared and be able to adapt to the discussion. Things that come out of the chat can change the data and make you have to change your arguments at the moment so you can handle it.

How does this apply to you?
The personality traits of a person determines their behavior, emotional approach and how they act in the professional, personal and family spheres. A person's personality consists of the characteristic ways in which he thinks, feels and behaves, making him unique. The theories about what is personality and how it develops are many. Creating and shaping a personality involves mainly biological and environmental factors.

The biological field includes genetic, hereditary factors. In the environmental field, the conditions in which a person grows, is raised, educated and lives is involved. It is not easy to precisely define the characteristics of a person's personality. Some of them are deeply rooted in their mental world and they are unchanged. Some others, probably based on his experiences. Unlike personality traits, an individual's skills and abilities are the result of the training he is undergoing. The experience added to the training strengthens the competence of a person in his / her field. Success in life, of course, requires training, experience and competence in the professional field of every person.

However, it is the personality that has a decisive influence not only on the quality of education and competence but also on how these necessary skills will be used in practice during the working life to lead to success.

There are certain personality traits, which are more frequent in people who achieve their professional lives. It is important to look at some of the most common and most important personality traits of successful professionals because we can draw some lessons that will help us achieve our goals over the long term:

Personality 1. Self-awareness
On the road to success is a prerequisite for someone to understand his strong and weak points, his interests, what he wants in his life, and how his fellow human beings and his family would like to see him. The "knowledge of it" is always a diachronic principle, which needs to be the experience of every man as to what he wants to achieve in his life.

Personality 2. Self-discipline
Without respecting the decisions taken by the person himself, there can be no successes for himself and for the achievement of his goals. In life too many are the temptations and distractions, distracting or stealing the precious time required to achieve the goals. He who can not self-discipline will not be able to reach his goals.

Personality 3. Self-confidence
Self-confidence must be based on solid and proven bases. Confidence is not easily obtained. It needs training and experience. Without success, there is no success. That's why a successful practitioner invests a lot, time and effort to acquire

it and cultivate it, because it will be an excellent tool in the struggle of life.

Personality 4. The enthusiasm for a vision
Individuals who have a vision of a particular subject, an idea or a social mission can inspire and sensitize and mobilize others with the enthusiasm that characterizes them. People can and feel the enthusiasm, interest, and faith that a person may have for realizing a vision, goal, or mission. Surely he, who can inspire others thanks to his measured, balanced and pure enthusiasm, but also thanks to his actions, will have a basic prerequisite to succeed.

Personality 5. Positive approach with optimism and positivity
Optimism and positive approach are key features of the personality of successful people in all areas of activity. The belief in a positive development of efforts to achieve a person's goals is usually accompanied by ways of thinking that help to overcome and effectively address the inevitable obstacles to any action required on the path to success.

Personality 6. Persistence accompanied by hard work, without impulsivity and patience
Difficulties, failures, hardships, bangs, and any obstacles, foreseeable or unpredictable, are an inevitable part of any human effort to achieve any important goal. The successful man can withstand. He knows well that obstacles will be created on the road, waiting for them and preparing to deal with them. The perspective analysis of the obstacles and the dangers that await it allows him to remain calm in adversity.

Personality 7. Ethics, consistent and honest
Consistency, sincerity, honesty, conscientiousness and sound principles of morality and law are essential components for a lasting and well-founded success in life. A successful person is fair with everyone, even when there is no one or it is impossible to control him. Success without justice and respect for one's fellow is not real, but worthless and transient.

Personality 8. Networking
Success in the life of every professional requires education, skills, abilities and competence in his field. However, networking at social and professional level is very important, with a huge role in achieving the goals. Networking, that is, the development and cultivation of constructive relationships with other people, aiming at pleasure and self-help is a fundamental feature of human society. Without proper social networking, chances of success in life are drastically reduced.

Personality 9. The commitment to the goal
Attention to the goal is a major feature of the personality of successful people. Knowing someone well what they want and what they are is the first step of the long and difficult road to success. The commitment to the goal, without disorientation and loss of energy in unnecessary movements, is a significant advantage of the personality of the successful.

Personality 10. Good listening to others and sympathy
The efficient practitioner knows and listens well and closely to his interlocutors. He knows that the people with whom he is in contact can be a source of knowledge and real treasures. Ability to understand and sympathize with others provides valuable services to the person who is thirsty for success.

Personality 11. Flexibility and versatility
The rigidity in life can be costly. But the same applies to flexibility. Adaptability is the ability of a person to change their mode of action or direction depending on what is happening to him. Choosing the right mix of flexibility and stiffness, depending on each problem, is a matter of individual personality judgment. It is this crisis, in relation to adaptability, that plays a key role in success in life.

It is, of course, impossible to define all the individual personality traits that lead a person to success.

However, studying and analyzing the way people think of successful people can offer a lot to everyone who is keen to succeed in their professional life. Once you can achieve this, persuasion is like a second skin for you.

Chapter 4
Persuasion techniques
Methods of persuasion are techniques in rhetoric that
determine the speaker's speech strategy when addressing
listeners. Aristotle, in his Rhetoric, describes the methods of
persuasion as follows. The methods of persuasion include
ethos, pathos and logos.

There are three types of ways of persuasion provided by
speech: some of them are determined by the nature of the
speaker, others by the mood of the listener, and others by the
speech itself with its true or imaginary conviction.

Ethos (temper)
Ethos  is an appeal to the authority of the speaker, as well as to
the moral values that audience members share in relation to
the subject of the presentation or conversation. If the speaker
knows or suggests that audience members have certain moral
values, he can refer to these values to support his ideas. In
order to do this, he must demonstrate how his idea is
consistent with these moral values. It is also important that
the speaker prove that he is fluent in the subject matter of the
speech. Being a prominent figure in the field under discussion,
for example, a professor in this science or a manager in this
industry demonstrating possession of a special "cargo" after
receiving a recommendation from a reputable person.

Pathos (mood)
Pathos is an appeal to the emotions of the audience. This
includes sympathy, pity and empathy. Pathos can be in the
form of a metaphor, comparison, passionate performance, or
even a simple statement that the issue has been resolved
unfairly. Pathos can be especially useful if used well, but most
speeches do not rely solely on pathos. Pathos is most effective
when the speaker demonstrates agreement with the basic
values of the reader or listener.

In addition, the speaker can use appeals to fear in order to
influence the audience. Pathos can also include calls for the

imagination and hopes of the audience; this is achieved in that the speaker draws a scenario of a positive future as a result of the proposed measures.

In some cases, the speaker resorts to lowering the ethos in order to isolate pathos - for example, William Jennings Bryan resorted to this technique in his speech about the golden cross.

It would be presumptuous of me to oppose the respected gentlemen whom you have just listened to if it were only about the art of eloquence; but we are not here a competition of personal qualities. "Even the most modest citizen of our country, dressed in the armor of justice, is stronger than those sets of absurdities that they have piled up here. I came to speak with you in defense of the same holy thing as freedom - in defense of human nature".

Logos (logic)
Logos is a logical attraction or its simulation. This method usually involves facts and figures in support of a speaker's statement. The use of logos also enhances the ethos method, as it emphasizes the speaker's awareness and preparedness for his or her audience. However, an abundance of data can also confuse the audience. The logo may also be misleading or inaccurate, although it may seem significant at the time of the performance. In some cases, inaccurate, fake or out of context data can be used to enhance the effect of the pathos. This is the case, for example, with a deliberately inflated or underestimated number of victims.

What is the difference between persuasion and suggestion? Persuasion is a term with two psychological interpretations. This element of outlook of the person for causing her to act in a certain way (for example - do not enter into an intimate relationship with a guy on a first date, because you should behave like good girl), and the transfer of world element to another person (for example - to convince her friend that the first dating - no sex, and only this is correct). This transfer of information or the attitudes to the addressee occurs in the process of education, when parents or teachers teach children to act honestly, to come to the aid of those who need it and to be useful members of society. In scientific debates, truth is born, too, thanks to the opponent's conviction in the veracity of the theory put forward. As a rule, the speaker's own point of view argues, and the listener interprets it and decides whether to agree with what has been said or not to agree. That is, it is a conscious process of perceiving information and accepting it as an installation of its own. In the process of persuasion, therefore, a person is born a new own conviction.

Suggestion is a different process. This is an aggressive psychological impact. Bypassing the consciousness and critical thinking of a person, they impose on him the attitude that he must fulfill. Suggestion occurs through the subconscious, and the inspired remains only to "blindly" absorb information. Suggestion occurs through hypnosis, pressure, or emotional-volitional effects. It is considered that it is possible to inspire something to a person mentally. The conclusions from the above are as follows: conviction is the conscious perception of information by a person, implying its comprehension, and suggestion is a bypass of critical thinking and an effect on the subconscious mind. Persuasion requires from those who wish to convey thoughts and attitudes of a great investment of time and effort, the suggestion happens faster and easier. Of course, you need to have the skills and abilities to the psychological effects of this kind.

Types of beliefs
So, we decided to influence the person, not bypassing his consciousness. How to convince? Repeat from the types of beliefs. This is a "base", after studying which, you can apply the techniques and methods to achieve the goal as quickly as possible.

Informing
The addressee is provided with full information about the object or phenomenon. If there are advantages, talk about them first. So the seller in the home appliance store tells the

buyer about the capabilities of the vacuum cleaner or hair dryer that interested him.

Clarification
This kind of belief is used when certain points need to be clarified. The same seller will decipher the technical characteristics of the power of the selected model to the buyer, translate the figures into the advantages that this vacuum cleaner has over other similar ones.

Evidence
It is addressed when data are requested to be accompanied by a visual representation or by real facts. So the chemistry teacher shows the children the Iodine Clock, demonstrating reversible reactions. The liquid in the flask becomes black, and when it is stirred, a transparent "water" is obtained.

Denial of
If the opinion of the convicted person is different from the one that he should have as a result of the impact, this type of belief is used. In other cases, the people themselves wish to receive a refutation of the information. So fans of the "Game of Thrones" are waiting for a denial of the death of John Snow in his favorite series. But neither the actors nor the project creators give it. This "framework" of persuasive influence is the base over which situational conditions are built. If the skills of the persuasive and the environment coincide perfectly and the addressee is ready to perceive information, the impact is doomed to success. Relaxed people and individuals who feel their similarities and those who persuade are easier to process.

Chapter 5
How to gain people's trust to manipulate their behavior
To enter into trust is to incline to your side, to arrange, to enter into "mercy". When they try to achieve this by cunning or flattering, they say that a person wants to rub in (sneak in) confidence.

Each person has their own individual style of behavior, facial expressions, gestures, body posture, intonation in the voice, the main set of verbal expressions, and of course the representative system. Every person has a certain system of worldview, perception of external reality and behavior. Knowing these features of the interlocutor, you can gain confidence in him while communicating with him using the technique of hidden manipulation of the interlocutor (neuro-linguistic programming - NLP), using the "tweaking" method. The fact is that people converge with others, guided by the principle of "common". It can be a mutual interest or a similar worldview, one zodiac sign or profession, similar facial expressions or a way to express one's emotions, etc. People love their own kind and reject "strangers." We are not interested in the interlocutor, in which with us there is nothing in common.

"Adjustment" is aimed at achieving subconscious trust with the interlocutor (rapport). The technology of building subconscious trust contains the following main components:

Adjustment to the pose
The first thing to do to build rapport is to copy the pose of your interlocutor. But this must be done naturally and easily, so that the interlocutor does not have the impression that the positions of his body are consciously copied. During the conversation, the partner may change the position of the body several times. Therefore, copying all the changes that occur in the position of his body, you need to follow them with a slight lag. To make the adjustment less noticeable, you can gradually adjust, for example, first make the same inclination of the body and head, and then adjust to the other positions.

Adjustment by gestures
Gestures are always a signal of any psychological changes in the interlocutor. By clearly adjusting the interlocutor's gestures system, one can achieve a deeper level of trust on the part of his unconscious.

To gain confidence in the interlocutor, it is not necessary to focus on exact copying of gestures, it is enough to reproduce their general direction. For example, if the interlocutor put his hand to his forehead, you can remove the imaginary mote from his jacket. If the interlocutor took off and rubs his glasses, you can manipulate the handle that lies before you.

Adjustment to breathing
This is a difficult technique to master, requiring a long workout. Adjusting to breathing means that we begin to breathe with the same depth and intensity as the interlocutor. In this case, it is better to begin to follow one thing, either inhaling or exhaling. An important feature of this technique is the ability to apply cross-adjustment, i.e., inhale-exhale; to reflect just not by his own breath, but by the movement of body parts, for example by tapping a finger on the table. In addition, in cases when it is physiologically difficult to adjust to the interlocutor's respiratory rate (who breathes too quickly or, on the contrary, too slowly), you can use the so-called method of multiple cycles. This method is that you need to breathe not synchronously with each breath and exhalation of a person, but skipping some cycles.

The greatest difficulty in adjusting to breathing is in recognizing how exactly the interlocutor breathes. A person's breathing can be heard, one can notice the breath of steam in the winter, and nostril movements in the summer. You can see how a woman's chest moves or a man's belly moves. You can hug or put your hand on your shoulder and enter the rhythm in this way.

It is necessary to note the aspect of the importance of exhalation. Since we are speaking mainly on exhalation, our internal speech is also synchronized with exhalation. Therefore, when you tune in to the interlocutor's breathing and speak on his exhalation, your speech will automatically adjust to the interlocutor's internal rhythm and increase the effect of psychological influence.

Adjustment under the speech
Adjustment to speech includes adjustment to the timbre of voice, speed of speech, and other characteristic features of the interlocutor's speech, for example, the use of parasite words and verbal predicates.

Theater reception
Consider a devastating technique with which you can instantly gain confidence in a person. This is a wonderful theatrical reception - echo. It consists in the repetition of words and phrases that the interlocutor uses in his speech. These words and characteristic turns can depend on various factors - on the profession, place of residence, occupation and much more.

What is the peculiarity of this method? Imagine that you are talking to the owner of a motorboat. If you call the subject of his pride "boat", then your chances of getting this boat for hire are drastically reduced to almost zero. Why? Yes, all because the owner will call her "ship"! And in order to effectively get in touch, you need to speak his language, because otherwise there will be a subconscious barrier between you and the interlocutor that will hinder the further development of the conversation.

How to inspire confidence and liberate the interlocutor? Speak in his language. Also, notice when someone speaks your language, because this is a professional who is familiar with this technique and wants to trust you and build good constructive communication and dialogue.

If a person calls his house "chalet", then he will not tolerate if you call him "house", so be careful. In fact, many kindergarten teachers are hard to bear when they are called "educators" because they are "preschool teachers"!

Speaking, notice the slang words with which a person characterizes the elements of his life, and then casually insert them into the conversation.

Psychological adjustment
This adjustment is implemented through the creation of a communication space in which you will feel with your interlocutor a part of one whole. At the same time, when it comes to methods of psychological adjustment, you should remember that entering the territory of maximum importance for another person and any wrong word or deed will immediately become an obstacle for you in further interaction with this person.

Adjustment for emotions
Before the start of exposure, it is advisable to bring yourself into the same emotional state as that observed with the interlocutor.

Adjustment to the structure of values
The values of another person are his rigidly fixed and definite attitude towards all things in the world. If suddenly there is a deep dissonance between your values - the person will be completely lost for you. Therefore, it is necessary to avoid any evaluative statements in the preparation and implementation of the impact. Evaluation statement activates the value structure of the interlocutor, and this very often leads to dissonance.

Adjustment to the representative system
Each person has a more developed one channel of perception. The main ones are: visual, auditory, kinesthetic. The dominance of a channel means that a person receives and processes information mainly in this form. From the dominant

perception system depends on the tactics of exposure to humans.

Among the signs of the domination of the visual channel is a lively look: the eyes are in constant motion, fast speech (a person does not have time to describe the images that arise in his head), in a conversation the following expressions slip: it ... "," I look at these things ... ", gestures in the upper body. The direction of eye movement: right - up (creating visual mental images), straight - up (remembering visual images), left - up (remembering visual images), straight - forward (figurative imagination from the memory or the outside world).

In the course of communication with the visual it is not necessary to tell him "listen to me", but it is necessary to say "look". You should rely on figurative comparisons, talk about "bright prospects", support his expectation of a "bright future."

A sign of the dominance of the auditory canal is a very pleasant, modulated voice with complex and diverse intonations. The following expressions are often found in speech: "I hear ...", "these are the sounds of my soul ...", "melody of life ...", "but I heard ...", "on hearing" ... Such people are very sensitive to the correct phonetic organization of speech, in particular to stresses. The direction of eye movement: left - sideways (recollection of sound images), left - down (internal dialogue with himself).

How to cause trust of such person? When communicating with the audial, maximum attention should be paid to the intonations of speech (raising or lowering the tone, changing the timbre, raising the volume, switching to whispers), since this will be the main instrument of influence.

For left-handers, this happens with the mirror opposite. In addition, there are some individual deviations from the general rules, and at different points in time the system of perception may change.

A sign of domination of the kinesthetic channel
A person operates with such concepts as feelings: "I feel this way …", "I felt it …", "oh, what feelings …", "I was caught up in this feeling …" attention to their comfort, selectivity in food, a great love for outdoor recreation. The direction of eye movement: straight - down (imagination of bodily sensations), right - sideways (creating internal sounds).

When communicating with kinesthetic, it is necessary to make more descriptions of possible sensations that may arise from the interlocutor during the interaction. For example, you can often say the phrase "you can feel that …", "a feeling of firm confidence." He needs to say "you feel," "feel," etc.

Approval
When a partner does or says something, he is always at a subconscious level waiting for an assessment of his actions. This is a very deep psychological mechanism, which is connected with the fact that any of our actions should automatically be evaluated by society. Using approval, you can push the interlocutor in the direction of the formation of his confidence in you. When entering into trust, consider the following.

Naturally, the subject's desire to establish rapport in all respects at once. However, this will lead to the fact that his brain will be overloaded with information. Instead of following the conversation thread, he will load the brain with such things as the need to avoid evaluative statements, etc. During the conversation, one must talk and not think about the individual components of how to create trust. Therefore, it is desirable to train the installation rapport strictly consistently. And while the subject does not bring one skill to automatism - you should not take up the next tool. It is a long way, but only it will lead to success.

In order not to look ridiculous and suspicious, it is necessary to act very subtly and carefully, without causing discomfort to the interlocutor. After all, frankly imitating, you can offend a person. In addition, it should be borne in mind that at first it is difficult to get used to this communication technique, but with practice it will become a habit.

Chapter 6
Techniques of persuasive conversation
Below we will look at ten effective persuasive conversation techniques that have been tested in practice by many professional negotiators, and then we will talk about the mandatory conditions and rules of persuasion, as well as the non-verbal component of persuasion and the most productive persuasive conversation behavior.

The negotiation techniques we consider include:

- Technique "Little moves"
- Power Shoulder Technique
- Technique "Internal Observer"
- Technique "If" instead of "No"
- Technique "Empty Cabinet Method"
- Technique "Gun always charged"
- Technique "There is no fixed prices"
- Technique "One Gate Game"
- Technique "Principle Method"
- Technique "Cool guys"

Technique "Little moves"
The "Little Movements" technique is a basic persuasive conversation technique. Its essence is to track the extent of its impact on the opponent by taking small steps and observing the reaction. Imagine, for example, what you say to your interlocutor:

 - Good day! Not so long ago I had a conversation with Sam Young, and he was telling you ...

The interlocutor may react completely differently, starting with surprise and ending with irritation, because he may not remember at all who Sam Young is, or he may decide that you gossip about him. It would be best to say:

- Good day! Just yesterday, we talked with Sam Young, and the conversation turned on you.

After that, it will be right to wait for the reaction of your opponent. A move can be strengthened if he answers you with something like:

- And, with Sam Young! Yes Yes...

If he begins to clarify what kind of person Sam Young is, then it is better to stop the development of the topic. In other words, the interaction should be built gradually: first, you make a small starting step, evaluate the reaction and only then do the next step.


Power Shoulder Technique
The Power Leverage technique is effective only in situations where one side has the ability to influence the decision of the other. To illustrate this technique, you can use the following metaphor:

A tortoise is swimming along the river, with a snake sitting on its back. A turtle thinks that if he throws off a snake, she will bite her, and the snake thinks that if she bites a turtle, she will throw her off.

In this case, if any party realizes that there is a power advantage on its side, constructive persuasive conversation can be forgotten - there will be manipulative conversations, during which the strong opponent puts pressure on the weak, waiting until he starts to retreat, or power negotiations with a pronounced strategy "WIN-LOSE".

Technique "Internal Observer"
The "Internal Observer" technique allows you to influence the persuasive conversation process, but only if you constantly monitor your opponent, trying to determine which persuasion strategy he adheres to.

If psychological pressure is exerted on you, and you still try to reach a compromise, your desire will be perceived as weakness.

In the persuasion process, you should always remain alert - be on your guard, i.e. use your internal observer , who will help you understand what is happening and will not let you lose sight of the moment when constructive negotiations (the WIN-WIN strategy) develop into destructive ones.

Technique "If" instead of "No"
Many have heard that professionals in everyday bargaining have the idea that the basic rule in any business communication is to say "No!". In fact, this is not quite the case: the main phrase of experienced negotiators is: "If ...".

- I'll lower the price a bit if you decide to purchase not one ... but two ...

"If I buy this camera, will you give me a case for him, too?"

Remember: a person who says "No!" Has a much lower chance of winning than a person who answers any question asked to him with the phrase "If ...", and the one who uses "If ..." often receives a much bigger reward than initially calculated.

Technique "Empty Cabinet Method"
The technique of "Empty Cabinet" is most often used in persuasive conversation, the purpose of which is to bring down the price of a product or reduce the cost of a contract. The meaning of the technique lies in the fact that you mentally open a cabinet in front of your opponent, showing that you do not have as many funds as he requests.

The goods you like are selling for 5,000 rubles, but you say that you only have 3,950 rubles in stock

As a rule, the seller in this case often makes a concession, because if the goods are not bought by you, he may not sell them at all. And remember one important rule in this technique: you do not have to accept a small discount offered by the seller. Remember: you have only 3950 rubles!

Technique "Gun always charged"
"The gun is always loaded" technique is a reflection of the main hunting principle, according to which the hunter always treats the gun as if it is loaded, even if there are no cartridges in it.

In the persuasive conversation process, form an idea in your mind, as if you already know that your opponent misunderstood you (or otherwise, but the opposite of the desired result), and get ready to take certain steps to eliminate this misunderstanding (think of an action plan)

Proceeding from this, if, following the results of the negotiations, you find that your opponent really did not understand you or did not understand you correctly, you will already be ready for this state of affairs - you will have a loaded gun at the ready - a plan of action .

Technique "There is no fixed prices"
Technique "There is no fixed prices" originates from a market economy. If you are familiar with this topic, then, of course, you know that fixed prices are a myth. Prices are always determined by how the supply and demand correlate with each other, as well as by how much the buyer wants to get a discount.

Let one of your rules be the rule of bargaining (and this may concern completely different areas and topics of negotiations). Bargaining is perfectly acceptable, correct and normal. The goal of any price tags is to impose on you that pricing policy that suits the seller. You have the full right to offer your price (the seller, in turn, has the full right to refuse)

Such negotiations, in which you begin to bargain, can bring you much more benefits than those in which you decide to be led by the seller (or opponent).

Technique "One Gate Game"
The "One Gate Game" technique says that you cannot make any concessions or make any special offers until you start bargaining. Any of your concession or special offer involves a concession or special offer from the opponent, and the proposal of the opponent should be more profitable than yours.

When you make a concession, take it for granted, and continue the conversation as if nothing much happened. Your main task in the persuasive process should be to achieve your goals.

The presented technique is very harmoniously combined with the "If" technique instead of "no".

Technique "Principle Method"
Technique "Method Principle" allows you to achieve your goals in persuasive conversation with minimal losses. The principal here is the person who has authorized you to take part in the conversations on your own behalf. Interestingly, your employer, a boss, a friend or a family member can act as a principal.

In the process of conversing, your opponent must understand that you are negotiating on behalf of another person, and also that you have specific conditions from which you simply cannot back down, because you do not have the right to do so.

In most cases, the use of this technique bewilders the opponent, as a result of which he is forced to agree to the conditions put forward by you. Please note that if this method is used against you, you can ask your opponent to connect you with the person on whose behalf he is negotiating.

Technique "Cool guys"

Technique "Cool guys" is used in cases where conversations are conducted with the "cool guys" themselves, who are trying to force you to accept their conditions, otherwise you will not be "fit".

When your opponent shouts, threatens to give you trouble, or swears in the hope that you will "limp" and fulfill his demands, you must remain cool. In no case do not enter into open opposition, do not give in to emotions, do not begin to argue on issues not related to the subject of discussions. As a result, "cool guys", most likely, "limp" themselves and will be ready to compromise.

Always remember that no matter how your opponent behaves, this should not affect the result that is planned to be achieved through negotiations.

The persuasion techniques that we have considered may seem extremely simple at first glance, because they lack piling up all sorts of cunning actions and sophisticated "spy tricks". But, if you recall one well-known truth, which says that everything that is most important is always on the surface, you will understand that the simpler the technique, the easier it is to apply, and the easier it is to apply, the more skillfully you can become a master of persuasive conversation.

But to think that everything to an extreme degree is trivial, also does not follow - this is a big mistake. Along with its simplicity, any persuasion technique, if it claims to be effective, must comply with the special conditions and rules, which we will discuss below.

Mandatory conditions for effective persuasion techniques
In total there are four mandatory conditions that must be met by any persuasive conversation technique:

The parties to the negotiations should be clearly defined. Simply presenting and sharing greetings and business cards will not be enough. A person becomes a subject of persuasion only when his opponent has given his consent to discuss the problem with him

A common agenda should be agreed. The agenda involves the formulation of explicit goals of opponents. But, given that they may have hidden goals, it is also very important to try to define and understand them. In the case when the common agenda is not agreed, the negotiators will lead them, guided by their own agendas.

Opponents must agree that negotiations are the main means by which they can resolve the situation that has arisen (remember the first lesson - the stage of preparation). Otherwise, it may turn out that one of the parties will either participate in the negotiations on coercion, or will not treat them with all seriousness.

Decision making should not be strictly regulated. Even the most serious negotiations may involve connecting to the search for agreement on creativity, the creative potential of the participants, etc. Strictly regulated decision-making conditions nullify any attempts to solve the problem in non-standard ways.

It is worth noting that these conditions, if they are not met, may also be peculiar barriers in the persuasion process. For this reason, they should be overcome at the very beginning, dotting all points above i.

Now let's talk about the rules of effective persuasive conversation techniques.

Mandatory rules for effective persuasive conversation techniques
According to the famous British diplomat and scholar Charles Eliot, there is no special secret in success in the process of interaction (business). The main thing is genuine attention to the speaker.

However, there are still a few rules that can make any persuasion technique successful:

- You must establish a good relationship with your opponent's employees (secretary, representative, etc.) You should always be punctual, because it will characterize you as a reliable person
- Try to minimize the impact on the negotiations of any third-party factors.
- Prepare for negotiations carefully and seriously.
- Strive to be an interesting conversationalist, and also show calm and sense of humor.
- In negotiations, be independent, collected and friendly; speak convincingly and clearly.
- Keep yourself in hand: avoid fuss, excessive zeal and annoyance.
- Try to smile more.
- Make sure that your opponent does not lead you to irritation and do not get confused.
- Let your opponent speak as much as possible. Listen to him carefully, do not interrupt.
- Have free access to all necessary materials and documents during negotiations.
- Use visual materials to support your words: charts, notes, tables, etc.
- During the conversation, use the terms and expressions that your opponent uses - what you say should be as clear as possible to your interlocutor.
- Speak specifically, pointing to facts, figures, details.
- In negotiations you must be energetic and persistent, but must also be correct and not try to break your opponent.
- Questions asked should be answered directly.
- Feel free to discuss sensitive issues and do not be afraid to engage in discussions.
- Use pauses in speech to make your words come to mind.
- Take the advice and help of your opponent willingly.

- Greater bias should be done exactly on the questions - this will allow you to enter a constructive dialogue and get the necessary information.
- Praise your opponent for his comments, encourage his comments with positive comments.
- Use feedback - watch how your opponent reacts to your words and what is happening in general.
- Pay due attention to all negotiators (write down the names of each of them at the beginning of the negotiations).
- Negotiations are more efficient to start not with the proposal of ready-made ideas, but with the analysis
- Try to "hook" your opponent, touching on the motives that guide him.
- Think about how this or that thought can be formulated in the best way (in some cases you should use special terminology, in others - simple words, in the third - comparisons and examples, in the fourth - experience, etc.)
- Voice your opponent the benefits he gains by agreeing with your ideas.

Here are a few additional recommendations that will be a very good addition to any strategy and negotiation technique you choose:

- Almost always, your negotiating opponent will have over-himself someone to whom he will later pass on your proposals. Proceeding from this, try to communicate your thoughts and arguments in an intelligible way, provide examples and convincing evidence.
- If your opponent makes impossible demands for you, reject them, but do not be arrogant and respect his dignity. You may well refer to a third party (principal) and indicate your obligations to him.
- The path of least resistance is the path of failure. Do not give such promises that you will not be able to fulfill. Your trump cards should be accuracy and veracity.

- Do not blindly believe all the reasons why they say no. Some of these reasons only sound convincing, but you should always be interested in the interlocutor, if he has some other reason why he behaves in this way and not otherwise.
- Do not be afraid to call your conditions, and do it intelligibly and convincingly.
- Any objections should be listened to absolutely calmly, avoiding emotional reactions.
- Always try to think about why your opponent may actually hesitate and hesitate.
- Initial attention should be focused on the positive sides of the negotiations and points of contact with the opponent. Any shortcomings and negative points need to be discussed after.
- Initially, be prepared for the fact that your opponent will have difficulty thinking about your proposals.
- When your opponent stops at any questions, agree with the fact that he acts reasonably.
- Feel free to ask counter questions to find out exactly what your opponent is referring to (among other things, this will allow you to gain time for an answer)
- Try not to enter into direct confrontation, and use the "Yes, but ..." method, offering your position instead of your opponent's position, but avoid categorical statements
- Ask your opponent to voice specific points of your proposals with which he agrees, and then ask again whether it is possible to come to an agreement on their basis.
- Do not avoid the use of concessions that can be perceived by the opponent well and encourage him to make a decision.
- Strive for high results - do not be satisfied with trifles, partial consents and small concessions.
- Always write down everything you promise to accomplish, everything you agree with, and everything you agree on. The negotiations should be guided by the

principle: the most blunt pencil is better than the sharpest memory.
- Controversial issues should be discussed at the end of the negotiations - after agreement has been reached on the remaining issues.
- When the negotiations will come to an end, ask directly: are there any more open questions? Is there any interference? What causes concern?

In addition to the above, it is worthwhile to talk about which behavior is the most productive in the process of negotiation.

The most productive behavior in negotiating
Considering the fact that this topic itself is quite large, we will give only a few of the most significant recommendations that you can rely on in any negotiations:

- You should always keep goodwill and imperturbability - this will protect you from any negative influences, both from your opponent and from the negotiation process in general.
- Make it a rule to always be an attentive listener. Also, do not forget about eye contact, but you should look, listening, not directly in the eyes, but on your opponent's lips.
- Apply conditional consent by, for example, an approving nod. Your opponent will take this as a signal indicating that you understand his point of view.
- Remember that the one who asks questions directs the conversation. Questions are a sign that a person has inner strength and sincere interest. And when negotiating with an aggressive opponent, more questions will soften his pressure.
- Look for contact points and general views.
- When you speak, look at your interlocutor - your words will be more expressive and convincing.
- Any person is subject to external influence, and he will willingly succumb to it if it plays into his hands, but begins to resist in every way if he feels that he wants to

be harmed in any form. For this reason, during the negotiation process, you should constantly ask yourself whether you see the situation sufficiently and whether your opponent sees the situation sufficiently.

But, as you know, people do not always say what they think, which means that you need to be able to somehow understand their thoughts and feelings, regardless of the words, i.e. to understand non-verbal communication, and it is here that nothing but methods and techniques of neuro-linguistic programming, about which we also say a little, but purely for informational purposes, can come to your aid .

Chapter 7
Non-verbal component of the persuasion
Mimicry and gestures of people can be considered the most accurate indicators of their internal state, desires and thoughts. The information that we can receive in this way should be perceived as more reliable than the information that comes from the words of our opponents, because in most cases the non-verbal component is controlled by the human subconscious.

Your success in persuasions will depend not only on what strategy you use, what techniques you use, and how competently you do it, but also on how developed your skill is in recognizing non-verbal signals. And this suggests that in the negotiation process you should pay attention to the poses, facial expressions and gestures of your opponents, as well as keep track of your own.

If you understand what your interlocutor is telling you through your facial expressions, gestures and postures, you can more accurately determine his position, attitude towards you, desire or unwillingness to find a mutually beneficial solution, etc.

In this chapter, we shall discuss the following:

- Persuasive listening
- Body language
- Exploiting the emotions of the interlocutor
- Get others to do what you want them to do
- Use the persuasion in marketing and sales

7.1 Persuasive listening
In fact, our brain is able to perceive the speed of speech six times higher than the average speed of the speaker. That is, the brain has a lot of time to "wander." Therefore, an active listener is one who knows how to concentrate intensively on what the speaker is saying and ignore all the parasitic thoughts that may distract him.

What to do during periods of inactivity of the brain? Summarize and absorb what you just heard. And also place each new piece of information in the context of what you heard earlier.

In addition to intense concentration, the transition to the "active listening" mode requires the manifestation of empathy. Thus, an active listener is one who enters the consciousness of his interlocutor in order to see his message from his point of view. He tries to feel the speaker's emotional, imaginary and cognitive universe in order to understand his views, his behavior and his system of values from within.

Also, the active listener refrains from judging the content of the utterance, which is not at all easy. Since it is natural for a person to be distracted from what the speaker is saying, especially when opinions diverge.

When someone hears what he does not approve of, he begins to mentally formulate opposing arguments, say the authors of the book Management, Basic Concepts and Practices. - By doing so, we do not listen to the rest of the utterance. Therefore, the task of the active listener is to carefully listen to the speaker, leaving his judgment for later.

In view of the foregoing, it is not surprising that people who use active listening methods are also (if not more) tired at the end of the meeting than the one who gave a speech. In other words, the energy spent on listening is equal to the energy spent by the speaker.

However, the game is worth the candle...

Successful leaders are often those who know the value of listening and those who seek to understand in order to be understood. Paradoxically, listening to someone else's opinion is usually the best way to convince the other person about his or her own point of view and make him see the world as we see it, says Dale Carnegie. - There is no more convincing person than an attentive listener.

He cites the example of Dean Ruska, Secretary of State President Johnson, who for many years held talks with the toughest world leaders: "Listening is a way to persuade others with your ears."

The American businessman Tom Saunders also spoke about this. He claimed that the secret of his success lay in his ability to listen. "It all comes down to hearing. What does my client really mean? Why did he say no? What is the real reason? What does he mean? What is he thinking about? How does he see it? "

In addition to business use, the method of active listening is very effective when communicating with a child. The famous child psychologist Julia Gippenreiter recently published a book called "The Miracles of Active Hearing". In it, she teaches parents how to make real and deep contact with the child. The book is full of concrete examples of life, it also has "homework" for parents.cActively listening to a child means "returning" to him in a conversation what he told you, while denoting his feeling, the author says.

Keys to a successful audition
However, most people try to convince others with their speeches, although this is counterproductive. Let others speak for your pleasure. They know their business and their problems better than you. If you do not agree with them, you will be tempted to interrupt them. But don't do it. Is it dangerous. They will not listen to you if they still have a lot of thought to dub.

What are the keys to a successful hearing? The Swiss company ProOptim  regularly conducts seminars on active listening and non-verbal communication. To show sincere interest in a conversation, an active listener must repeat and rephrase the speaker's words. He may also ask additional questions, if

necessary, to clarify some point. In addition, he finds
conflicting statements in the speaker's speech, prompts him to
continue the presentation and resists the temptation to
complete the sentences for him. Finally, he is looking for
visual contact with the interlocutor and uses some non-verbal
signals, such as a nod.

We devote years to learning to read and write, we also need
years to learn how to speak. Do we ever learn to listen?

7.2 Body language
How to learn to understand people, relying on their gestures
and facial expressions? The psychology of facial expressions
and body gestures provides an answer to this question. Having
studied and understood this topic, you can ensure the absence
of secrets and hidden meanings in conversations with others
and learn to read people like an open book.

Agree, the ability is very useful in persuasions, right?

Psychology of facial expressions and gestures. What is it?
Facial expressions and gestures in communication with others
play a huge role. They help to strengthen, fully reveal the
feelings. With the help of facial expressions, we express
emotions that we don't talk about. Our body is very cunning,
we can not notice, as we say one thing, and body language
shows something completely different. Without noticing
ourselves, we give out our hidden intentions and unsaid
words. Our body is more eloquent than any speeches and
tirades.

An inexperienced person will have a hard time figuring out
where and how his interlocutor had mislead him. But those
who are familiar with the subject of facial expressions and
gestures are provided with an understanding of the situation
and an opportunity to take it under control.

Facial expressions and gestures are very closely intertwined,
therefore they are always considered in one bundle. "He who

lies in the language of words, impersonates himself in sign language to which he pays no attention." - Oswald Spengler.

Terms and concepts of facial expressions and gestures
These are difficult to perceive for people who first come across the subject of gestures and facial expressions. Simply put, these are the components of a section of psychology, which make it possible to understand facial expressions and gestures at a more detailed level than "his ears are burning, which means he is lying". Everything is much more deep and serious than it might seem at first glance.

The dictionary of the symbolism of psycho anatomy is a kind of decoding of sign language. Based on it, you can find out what certain gestures mean in the current situation. This section is considered purely with specific examples, since in different situations, the same gesture can be interpreted differently. The ergonomics of facial expressions and gestures is a section that describes the ability to adapt body language to solve specific problems. For example, to influence the human psyche through positive beliefs transmitted through gestures.

Learning the ergonomics of gestures is a great way to learn how to communicate more productively and efficiently. It gives an opportunity to influence a person with gestures and facial expressions, which subconsciously cause positive emotions in him.

This is well used by scammers. For example, in order to arrange a person for himself, a scammer may touch his hand while telling a joke or some pleasant and funny story. Thus, the human brain begins to respond positively to this gesture. Then, when it comes to the "twisting" of the scam itself, the fraudster casually touches the hand of a person, awakening in his mind relaxation and positive. So it is easier to commit fraud, because a relaxed person will not begin to suspect something. His brain is deceived by psychology.

What gives an understanding of facial expressions and
gestures?
The active work of the brain
You need to remember a bunch of gestures and movements
that indicate a specific meaning. For example, if during the
dialogue the interlocutor scratches his head, it means that he
is not sure about your words and gives them doubt. One can
cite a lot of such examples, and most of them must be
constantly kept in memory.

The ability to adapt and change the situation
When you know more than you are told, you can often find the
right solutions in different situations, lead the interlocutor to
something or get answers where he doesn't even pronounce
them.

Understanding the negative motivations of a person
Knowledge of this topic will give you the opportunity to
protect yourself from lies, envy, unfriendliness, etc.

Understanding the inner world of the interlocutor
The correct interpretation of facial expressions and gestures
not only provides an opportunity to look into the soul,
revealing all the secrets of the interlocutor, but also
understand that he needs help, although he tries to hide it. In
this case, you can try to find the right words and try to deal
with the problem together.

The development of the ability to notice the smallest details
Without this ability it is impossible to interpret the current
picture of facial expressions and gestures. One unsung gesture
can drastically change the whole meaning of the signals given
by the body. Therefore, if we want to correctly interpret the
body language of another person, we need to be more attentive
and receptive to trifles.

Self-development
Self-development is an added bonus when studying the
psychology of facial expressions and gestures. A person learns

to learn both himself and those around him, studies something deep, draws something useful for himself.

How to start learning the language of facial expressions and gestures?
Consider all the sources of knowledge on the psychology of facial expressions and gestures:

Literature.
The first assistant in the study of this topic. In addition to printed books, many experts in this section of psychology publish magazines, open websites and blog on the Internet.

Courses on the study of the psychology of facial expressions and gestures.
A person who understands the topic will be able to personally show and explain how everything works and how to apply this knowledge in life.

View TV shows or documentaries on the subject.
Oddly enough, from there you can gather a very large amount of information. Plus, there everything is shown in practice, which greatly simplifies the understanding and assimilation of "lessons" in my head.

Practice.
Reading and watching is, of course, good, but it is necessary to apply this knowledge in real conditions. This is the only way to assimilate information and change something in your life.

Gestures and facial expressions - their significance.
Theoretical knowledge should be considered in specific, modeled situations. Only in this way can one correctly understand what the interlocutor "is silent" about. Let us analyze how the interlocutor's feelings are connected with the movements of various parts of his body.

Lips
Self-confidence is most often associated with lip mobility.

Example 1
The interlocutor, leaning his elbow on the arm of the chair,
pulls his lip with his index finger, while not making a single
sound.

This means that a person is confused and does not know what
decision to take. The interviewee thinks that they are trying to
manipulate, and his gesture is tantamount to insecurity. This
example is not frequent, but very eloquent.

Example 2
Her companion's lips, compressed, completely ceased to be
visible.

Here are two options:
It shows a person has a virtue, rather experienced, wise.

Disgust. And close to complete rejection. This is a more
frequent option.

In this case, the context of the conversation is important. If
you talk about something unpleasant during a conversation or
touch a topic that is painful to your interlocutor, you can
notice it by his tight lips. In this case, it is worthwhile to divert
the conversation aside and change the subject to a neutral one.

Example 3

The interlocutor bites the upper or lower lip.

This means a person's discontent. Your partner may be
exhausted and emotionally overwhelmed. If a woman bites her
upper lip, she is usually afraid of something.

Also this gesture can be considered as seduction, then it
testifies to love excitement.

Back

The back is the center of sensuality, also responsible for the ability to invest maximum strength in some business.

Example 1

The interviewee clapped a friend on the back.

This is a direct expression of sympathy or just a good mood. They say this is a shortened version of hugs.

It should be noted that this gesture does not always mean something good.

Example 2
The interviewer communicates with you, turning his back.

If men take this posture, this indicates their inability to make decisions. It also indicates a lack of leadership qualities, because the one to whom they are inherent will openly meet any turn of the situation and solve questions, being in person to the interlocutors.

Hands
The most active and mobile part of the body, it can tell a lot.

Example 1

If your partner keeps the brush in the pose of "prayer", then this means an implacable gesture rather than an indulgent one. It is necessary to be prepared for the fact that the interlocutor will object about what you said.

Example 2

The interviewer closes the hand, as if holding something small in it.

This gesture means that a person only takes, not gives. It is a symbol of selfishness.

The Jaw
The jaw is associated with anger in all its negative manifestations.

Example 1
Does it happen that a person in the middle of the night starts to grit his teeth? So, this is not at all a habit or a peculiarity of an organism, it is nothing but anger. Most often, a person who has experienced a very vicious and gloomy situation during the day, involuntarily manifests this at night through a dream.

Example 2
The interlocutor's jaws are constantly in a hidden chewing process. This indicates a very changeable personality.

Example 3
The nodules pulsate like under the skin, and tears are about to spill out of the eyes. This is a sign that the interlocutor is clearly losing his composure, he is something very shocked and holds emotions in himself from his last strength.

Under body language we consider only the main examples, besides them, the psychology of facial expressions and gestures deals with many situations and contexts. Thanks to this knowledge, everyone has the opportunity to feel the essence of the behavior of his interlocutor, to understand what he really is experiencing and feeling. Sadly, people tend to lie, to hide something or keep back. The psychology of facial expressions and gestures will help shed light and clarity on many situations, such serious knowledge can save you from trouble.

How to use the knowledge of body language?
You can use this knowledge very actively.

If it was noticed by certain gestures or facial expressions that the other person does not wish to continue the conversation, you can tactfully end the conversation and leave. Watching a new acquaintance cunning or hiding the truth, you can remove such a person from the social circle, depriving yourself of eternal secrets and omissions.

You can escape from deceivers.
Professional liars and manipulators are well versed in psychology. In order to hide the secret manifestations of facial expressions or gestures, they learn to control the smallest movements.
They are hard, but still possible to get to the core. It is enough to watch their behavior for some time, somewhere their body will fail and then everything will become apparent.

Tip: if you are not sure of the truthfulness of the person's speeches, ask him more questions and watch his body movements.

Such deep knowledge makes it possible to see the true face of people. Not everyone is who they say they are. So why not "split" a person before he could take something not very pleasant in your direction.

On the positive side, the ability to use gestures and facial expressions can subconsciously arrange a person for you, relax him and make him very compliant. You can positively influence him, his well-being. So why not make a person's emotions positive, using his body language and yours?

In summary, the psychology of body language mastery is not an easy topic to learn and master. But how interesting and exciting it is! Just think, the interpretation of simple elements of behavior help to literally read a person like a book. This is a very valuable ability. First of all, it comes with the ability to observe. It is not necessary to be a graduate or have a long work experience in this field. It is enough just to learn to see, notice all the little things and analyze them, scroll through the facts in your head, compare information and draw conclusions.

The psychology of facial expressions and body gestures can teach you to see people through and through. This is a real superpower, which can only be possessed by a person with great persistence and desire to comprehend the secrets of human psychology and use it to his favor.

7.3 Exploiting the emotions of the interlocutor
When talking, people are constantly gesticulating without even realizing it. So, gestures are the key to the emotions and intentions of the speaker. Want to immediately reveal the secrets of others? As noted in 7.2, then learn to recognize body language.

What do hand movements mean
Gestures are a "window" into the world of a person's true thoughts, since consciousness does not follow them as strictly as, for example, behind words. From the movements of the hands, one can understand how a person treats what he says: positively or negatively, whether he likes it or not. Scientists reviewed and dismantled the speeches of politicians (2,000 gestures and 3,000 statements were analyzed): it turned out that, speaking of something good, right-handers tend to gesticulate with their right hand, and when they talk about something bad, with their left. For left-handers, the opposite is true: the left hand is associated with the positive, the right hand with the negative.

So if you want to understand what the speaker himself thinks about his words, watch your hands. The only thing you need to be aware of, he is right-handed or left-handed. However, as a rule, it is easy to find out: we know in advance what kind of hand is leading from family, friends and colleagues, and if we don't, it's enough just to watch. As for public persons, the Internet will help you.

How can you apply this in life and work? Very simple. Keep in mind that right-handed people are more likely to agree with people who are actively gesticulating with their right hand, while left-handers agree the opposite. Get to know your audience better - the people with whom you often communicate: clients, colleagues, students, if you are a university teacher. Do you think this stuff? But sometimes they decide everything. Suppose you come to an interview: here your task is to make the best possible impression on the employer. So why not pick up an ace in the hole in such a case?

How to find out your gift
How a person takes an object depends on how he is going to use it. So you can recognize intentions, that is, what a person will do with the subject further, and also find out whether he likes this "something" or not. Suppose we take the same bottle from the table differently depending on what we are going to do with it - drink water or throw it in the trash. In the same way - according to the principle of convenience for further actions - people take light bulbs, tennis balls, plates. Interestingly, monkeys do the same thing as humans.

But back to how to determine whether a person liked the thing or not. Imagine that you came to a friend's birthday party and gave him a gift. And now watch ... If he takes it as if he is going to use it right away, then everything worked out - the surprise was a success. If not, then maybe you missed the idea. Although do not worry: after all, gestures are not the only indicator of sympathy for the subject.

How to recognize anxiety
Smooth gestures are another "signal flag", always pay attention to them. Professional poker players train for many hours a day to do an indifferent facial expression (the so-called "poker face") - by their facial expressions you can't understand anything. But traitors are hand gestures. Self-confidence makes hand movements smoother, softer and slower. Scientists have found that poker players who moved chips more calmly had stronger cards in their hands. Simply put, they were almost sure of their winnings. Whatever you do with your body, and especially with your hands — accompanied the story with gestures or simply took care of a piece of paper — everything that is on your mind is reflected in it. That is why in

the right situations, follow the smoothness of your own gestures and, of course, look closely to those around you.

Do you want to know if something really bothers you? Often, the consciousness does not miss traumatic experiences, and then we can begin to feel bad, because emotions do not get out. In the book "The brain in a dream," the advice of Allan Hobson, a famous dream researcher, is given: reflect on the content of your dreams (the plot, scenes and heroes of dreams will help - the brain doesn't choose them by chance) and understand exactly what is bothering you.

Is the interlocutor trying to dominate?
Open postures of the body, with wide gestures of hands, indicate that a person feels strength and control over the situation: arms raised to the sky, arms spread wide with clenched fists, legs spread are all signs of dominance. Demonstrating self-confidence, a person tries to take with the body as much space as possible. The most interesting thing is that such postures not only translate the idea of self-confidence to others, but also make the person himself even more feel his stable position. Often, body position (especially) affects the outcome of the discussion or negotiations: even in a telephone conversation, posture is important. Keep this in mind when you meet with colleagues or business partners. However, do not forget one more thing: such open poses can certainly help win, but many perceive them as an excessive demonstration of strength, aggression and even the intention to deceive, to behave as something unethical. That is why use such a pose with caution - and the opposite is true: according to research, people who like to accept it are more likely to cheat and violate established rules.

Psychologists from Princeton University, USA, took photos of famous tennis players of the level of Maria Sharapova after victories or defeats in important matches and asked volunteers to guess what emotions athletes are experiencing. It is important that some photos were even without a face - only the body. To the surprise of scientists, the subjects more accurately determined their emotions when they saw a pose, even in spite of mimicry. So exercise - and then you will be able to quickly recognize emotions, better understand those around you and reveal their true intentions.

7.4 Get others to do what you want them to do
Here, we use the experience of a former hostage rescue specialist. He explains how to pull anyone to his side.

Mark Goulston has played many role-playing games in the past two years. He portrayed a suicidal policeman holding a pistol at his neck and threatening to pull the trigger. The training was attended by FBI agents and police officers whose task was to dissuade him from suicide. "At the end of the game, I usually pulled the trigger and then explained that I had to ask or say to make me retreat from my plans," explains Goulston, a former FBI agent and an expert on the release of hostages. Today, Goulston, business consultant and bestselling author, "I Can Hear You Through - Effective Negotiation Technique" uses in its trainings these tips for managers of large corporations like GE, IBM and Goldman Sachs, the experience that he gained while working at the FBI.

Gowston shared a few tips on how to get people — clients, colleagues, employees, or even bosses — to do what you need.

They must speak
After you have asked for something - or subtly hinted that you would like - stop and let the person say what he wants. "As soon as he starts talking, he will discover for himself the urgency of what you are asking of him," explains Goulston. The person himself will decide what to do what he is asked for without your persuasion. If you say only you, people will simply stop paying attention to your words or will perceive it as if they are given instructions and they don't want to do what you want.

Pay attention to adjectives and adverbs in the interlocutor's speech

"An adjective is a way to decorate a noun, and an adverb is a way to decorate a verb. And both of these parts of speech characterize your interlocutor's emotional background, "explains Goulston. After the other person has spoken - even if he asked you a question - pause, and instead of answering, respond like this: "Hmm ..." (This will signal that you heard it and think it over.) And then say something about the adjective or adverbs that the interlocutor used. This will help you to understand what is really significant for him, and will induce the interlocutor to pay more attention to the negotiations, which means that he will have more interest in helping you.

For example, if the person talking to you uses the adjective "wonderful" in relation to some solution and then asks you a question, try to respond like this: "I can answer your question, but tell me about this wonderful option first". This will force the person to open up to you at a deeper level than when you simply answer the question asked. "The more your interlocutor discovers to you, the more attentively he will listen to what you say," says Goulston.

Encourage "fill in gaps"
"By asking someone a question, you immediately trigger unconscious memories of how a person was once put in a difficult position by his parents, teachers, or coaches, and thereby put yourself in opposition to the interlocutor," says Goulston. Then the person reflexively steps back.

To avoid this, insert your questions or ask to "fill in the blanks," advises Goulston. For example, when you ask the question "What will you do about situation X?", You kind of hint: "You better know the answer, or else ..." This provokes confrontation. It is better to ask in another tone - "I want to know": "And do you plan to undertake about this ...?"

With this approach, you involve the person in the sentence you uttered, and do not ask a question that pushes the interlocutor to think that you are against him.

Access positive memories.
Believe it or not, almost every time you ask a person to do something, you trigger unconscious memories. "And the trick is to run positive, not negative," advises Goulston.

If a person associates your request with something positive, he will be more inclined to fulfill it. Once, Goulston asked one of her clients why she chose him over a woman coach. She replied: "You are like an elder brother to me, which protects me, clever, cheerful and slightly disrespectful - and when you point me to something that should be changed in my life, instead of arguing, I listen to you and go contact because I feel love and warmth in your words. "

Do not overtighten the blanket.
A good way to get people to do what you need is to make them feel important. People fall into two categories, says Goulston: some, sympathetic, develop the words of the interlocutor and add something to them, others drag the blanket over themselves and either seize the initiative to talk about themselves or try to put themselves above the interlocutor. "Well, it looks like you took a good trip to Florida. But we went to Fiji. "

The first ones give the interlocutor to feel that his words are important, but from the second one there is the impression that they are listening only in order to speak, or even belittle a person.

For example, a sympathetic person will say: "What a cool idea! Clever and creative. We can even move on and make X if this, in your opinion, works. " And the one who pulls the blanket over himself will answer: "You have a good idea, but I actually told my boss my version, and he liked it, so it's probably better to do as I suggested."

Focus on the future.
People don't like critics. They begin to defend themselves when you make out the situations in which they failed, says

Goulston. So if you want a person to act differently in the future, do not focus on the past. Better say: "I want to say that in the future I will be very grateful if you could do this, this will be very useful for the whole team."

"Make it clear to the interlocutor that you appreciate his efforts, explain why this is important to you. This allows people to feel that they are making a significant contribution to the common cause, "explains Goulston.

When you try to convince people, most often they feel that you are trying to put pressure on them, says Goulston. If you focus on what they would like to hear, they will be much better off taking your thoughts.

7.5 Use the persuasion in marketing and sales
Only if you yourself want it, will you buy something somewhere. All right. But didn't it happen that you didn't plan to buy any kind of thing, but in the end you didn't have enough money and did it voluntarily? And about any hypnosis and other "magic" of speech did not go. You may not even recognize such a fact, but almost certainly you, like, apparently, all the people on the planet, were subject to a hidden effect, the purpose of which is to convince you to perform a particular action.

We have a club of smart retailers here, so the action in question is a purchase. The impact itself is based on a number of simple and understandable psychological tricks, which are described in this final aspect of this chapter.

Rhetorical questions.
A rhetorical question is one that does not require an answer. Rhetorical questions that imply the answer "yes" are actively used in marketing and sales: "Do you want to be healthy?", "Do you want a new car?", etc. A positive response is the first step towards buying / selling. Then it will be easier to give and receive yes answers. In the absence of direct face-to-face communication, the online seller can use rhetorical questions

in the descriptions of their products. For example, a description of a toy in an online store may begin with the words "Did your child deserve a gift?". we use online stores as an example, as you find it even more difficult to convince people that you cannot see. however, all of the steps listed here are applicable to face-to-face scenarios.

Flattering.
People love flattery. Hearing something like "You deserve this [product name]," a person is inclined to agree with such a statement, because it distinguishes it from a number of others, gives it some significance. In marketing, more often use statements that highlight the good qualities of a person: "You value quality," "You only need the best", etc. Compliment as such, almost without fail, has a listener to the one who expresses it, which has a positive effect on further communication. The main thing, of course, is not to overdo it. In the context of an online store, flattery can be used both on the product pages (again, "You deserve ..."), and in greetings, shop description ("Best for the best", "For the sophisticated").

Simplification
Luring John Sculley to Apple, Steve Jobs asked him this question: "Do you want to sell sweet soda all your life, or are you ready to come with me and change the world?" Jobs has clearly simplified the real situation: working as a PepsiCo president means only selling carbonated drinks. In addition, Steve reduced the choice to two points, and colored them so that one of the options looked like a dull continuation of the routine, and the second - an adventure of a lifetime. In an online store, simplification can work well as a final incentive, the final push to buy. Accordingly, it is better to place a "simplifying" phrase somewhere closer to the "Add to cart" button (for example, "You can continue working on your buzzing laptop or become the owner of a new [name of the top model]").

Restriction

"Only until the end of the month", "only from such and such on such and such date", "only to the first ten customers" - such phrases are often used in advertising of various actions and sales. Their action is based on a simple human reflex: if the resource is limited, you need to have time to grab a piece of it. The realization that the opportunity may be missed leads to a kind of panic, and panic is able to successfully deal with common sense. Of course, we are talking about a slightly interested audience. Men limited in time discounts on feminine hygiene products are unlikely to lure. In Internet commerce, the restriction can be used in the same way as in ordinary advertising: notify your visitors about the limitations of the offer using a large banner or red numbers in the "Left in stock:" line and evaluate the result.

Comparison
Some engines of online stores allow you to indicate in the product card not only its actual price, but also the previous price. Usually, the previous price noticeably exceeds the current offer, which pushes the consumer to compare, conclude on how profitable a deal is offered to him and (in an ideal scenario) to buy a product. It is worth noting the combination of "restriction + comparison" tricks, often used by TV shops: you are shown something, paint it beautiful and useful, and by the time you already believe that this thing is not enough in your life, you are finished off with the phrase in the style: "Call and order right now, and get a dizzying discount of so many thousand rubles." And give a superterk as a gift, naturally. Judging by the fact that tele-sales have been around for decades, this combination works more than well.

Total: knowledge is power, but this force should be used with caution. The techniques described in these few pages require modification in each specific situation, and with successful decisions they can have a very positive effect on the sales of your store and business in general.

Chapter 8
The Chameleon effect
In a store-based experience, salespeople did or did not imitate the verbal and non-verbal behaviors of clients. It seems that mimicry is associated with an increase in the rate of purchase, more conformity with a suggestion made by the seller and more positive evaluations of the seller and the store. The mediation analyzes have highlighted the role of the seller's perception of skills in the relationship between mimicry and buying behavior. The managerial interest linked in particular to the training of the salesmen and to the importance of the customer / seller relationship is important.

In psychology, there is a great variety of syndromes and effects. Many people use the metaphor in their name to refer to the explanation of the effect. Examples include Peter Pan syndrome, Jerusalem syndrome, Othello syndrome, Benjamin Franklin effect, Mandela effect, etc. If we had to put one forward, it would be the chameleon effect.

Chameleons are small scale reptiles with large, colorful eyes and extensible tongues. They are very characteristic in the eyes of the general public for their ability to change their skin color. Nevertheless, the popular conception of the fact that they change their color to camouflage is not completely accurate. Similarly, the chameleon effect does not indicate that people change color but the way they change.

Chameleons changing color
Only some species of chameleons have the ability to change color. Chameleons are not colorless and their color changes do not always occur in harmony with the environment. The majority of color changes are due to a physiological condition. Chameleons react to temperature and time of day by changing color. The color also changes in other situations because of the presence of psychological factors. For example, facing an opponent or a partner. In the struggles between chameleons, they also change color. The color indicates if the chameleon is

angry or scared. The color change is sometimes also a means of communication between chameleons.

People changing color
In a film by Woody Allen, Zelig, a very strange character appears. Performed by Woody Allen in person, the main character Leonard Zelig appears in different places and interacts with different people. So far, everything is normal but Zelig presents each time a different aspect. When he is with black people, his skin color and voice change. When he meets Jews, his beard grows and English people appear in his hair. When he is in the company of heavier people, his weight also increases.

This strange case is studied by Dr. Eudora Flechter, interpreted by Mia Farrow. The doctor manages to discover in Zelig an extreme case of insecurity that leads him to camouflage himself among people by adapting his appearance to be accepted. Zelig has the supernatural ability to change his appearance by adapting to the environment in which he evolves, which gives him the name of chameleon man. After lying about reading a book, Moby Dick, his need for acceptance to feel included leads him to change physically and psychologically.

"You are like the chameleon who changes according to the occasion." - Zelig

Obviously, Woody Allen's film is a parody or tries to be by the search for caricature. It shows an impossible situation which, faced with the metaphor, can lead to a better understanding of what the chameleon effect is. This effect is also called emotional contagion and is based on the tendency to feel and internalize emotions similar to those we see and in the same way, to condition those of others. It is a process in which the person is influenced and at the same time influences the emotions and behaviors of other people or groups.

The chameleon effect explained

The chameleon effect defines a reality, that of the fact that in a certain way we all function as if we were a mirror for other people. We imitate the emotions of others or at least the emotions that unconsciously we think others express. This effect does not stop there, we also imitate postures and facial expressions, language, tone, accent and vocabulary.

Our natural reaction when someone is having a laugh is laughing too. When we are surrounded by people whose accent is different, we usually do not delay. If we sit with someone who crosses our legs, we will probably end up sitting in the same way. Although this effect does not always occur, it appears very often, as well as a conscious form, or as an unconscious form.

Function of the chameleon effect
The function of the chameleon effect, from an evolutionary perspective, was sensed by Charles Darwin. The actions we take determine in part how we feel. In the same way, the signals emitted by other people will influence us. This allows the personal well-being to be bigger and it also allows us to integrate within the groups. Without realizing it, small signals from others show us how to act and our mirror neurons allow us to imitate them.

We may all have a Zelig in us. When we are with other people, we adapt ourselves to have the same emotional state as they do. The emotions are like a virus, they transmit to our surroundings. We are programmed to contaminate and be contaminated by emotions from birth. If you live positive emotions, others will also feel them. If, on the contrary, you feel negative emotions, others will feel them in the same way. Although this process is unconscious for a good part, you can take the first step with your positive emotion.

"I'm like a chameleon, influenced by what's going on. If Elvis can do it, I can do it. If the Everly Brothers can do it, Paul and I can do it. The same thing with Dylan." -John Lennon.

Chapter 9

Learn a few "hacks"

9.1 Saying the right words at the right time

For centuries, people have been trying to comprehend the science of the word in order to become the best speakers, have an influence on people through the word and overcome the problems in communicating with people. PhD instructor, writer and motivational speaker Harry Segal helps people achieve these goals. In his book, he gives a lot of examples from life, where he describes how to act, and how not to; shows a variety of ways to solve social problems through communication.

I will give you tips from the book, applying which you can develop confidence and skills in convincing the interlocutor, as well as select words that create the best impression of you. You will feel easy to communicate with "difficult" people, and overcome the problem of "closure" during a conversation.

Tip number 1: "Choose your words carefully. Avoid unnecessary speeches, introductions and conclusions."

Before important meetings and speeches, we usually prepare a speech, think about what to say and what is better not to say, but we can never predict at what point our brain will give one or another phrase that will compromise us. How often we begin our speech with the words: "You know, I did not have time to prepare and I am not a master to speak at such a crowded meeting, but ...". With this phrase, we convince listeners that an amateur stands in front of them. Or in a conversation can slip: "I, in your opinion, an idiot?!". The interlocutor's thoughts after this will surely slip: "where did he get that I consider him an idiot, well, if he said so, then so be it".

Tip number 2: "To make people really listen," hook "the listener, summarize the information and give him only the essence, summarize what was said, create a convincing and memorable message from those words that are clear to the listener, do not enter him into a situation in which he will have to think a lot about your speech and translate it into his own language. ”

The human brain is so constituted that it responds only to what is available to it, understandable and interesting. If the interlocutor talks for a long time about the problem of lack of fresh water, while going into all the details, he will only listen to you if his area of interest is related to your narration. Otherwise, the interlocutor's brain switches automatically to other thoughts due to the fact that he cannot “process” your words.

Tip number 3: “Avoid statements based on “you,” as well as words like “forever,” “never,” “ should.” Replace statements about “you” with statements about “yourself.”

Any negative information about the interlocutor, which comes from your mouth to him, puts a block in the health of further conversation. Whatever you say after criticism will be perceived negatively, even if after criticism you say neutral or positive things. To avoid such a situation, try to beat the phrase so that it sounds like a description of you, and not the other person. Do not say "you upset me," better "I was upset."

Tip number 4: “In order to convince the interlocutor, in any case, do not tell him about his wrongfulness. First agree with him, and then offer to make corrections in his idea.”

For example, if you have a difficult conversation with management, you are at great risk of being wrong (according to management). To do this, after listening to all the suggestions and recommendations of the chief, you can agree with him with the phrase "I understand why you think so" or "In your place, I would perhaps take the same decision," and then tactfully say to him: “May I share an alternative view of the situation with you? ”

According to Allan and Barbara Pease, renowned experts in the field of non-verbal communication, a person with stronger arguments usually wins over telephone conversations, but if the negotiations are carried out personally, then everything happens differently, because, in general, we make the final decision on the basis of what we see rather than what we hear. This suggests that in a personal conversation, non-verbal signs that we give each other have a huge influence on the final decision. Therefore, in order to have an advantage in a conversation over the interlocutor, Segal gives the following advice:

Tip number 5: "When sitting, sit up straight."

Tip number 6: "Look people in the eye."

Tip number 7: "Record yourself in the video to" catch "all the movements that spoil your appearance."

Tip number 8: "When talking on the phone, use a mirror. Be aware of your offense or anger. If you do not want to show these emotions, put your thoughts in order, and then your appearance. "

Tip number 9: "Before you meet with the always dissatisfied client or employee," rehearse "your appearance. Create an image that you want to match, so that your body reflects your thoughts. When we are confident that we are doing the right thing, our body is in harmony with our thoughts. When we think that we are doing something bad, the body betrays us. So, before you start a conversation, check your thoughts and prepare physically. "

And finally, a tip that will help you not to get into unpleasant situations due to excessive talkativeness:

Tip number 10: "Conduct an experiment: try to remember almost every word you uttered in the last 2-3 hours. If you had the opportunity not to say any of this, would you do so? If so, be careful with your every word. Do not allow the uttering of words that you will later regret. ”

Learning to speak beautifully: 6 mistakes in conversation
You think you speak great and can communicate with people? Maybe everything is not as good as you think ... But I am ready to help.

1. Word-parasites and tautology
The other day, you know, uhh ... there was this, when I spoke, I tried to say something and just could not say anything, because well ... I don't know, it just doesn't come to mind.

Compare with this option:

The other day I could not speak, because nothing came to mind.

And with this:

Last week, during a conversation with a potential client, I could not even say a word, because my head was empty.

What example do you think is more successful and more likely to attract people's attention? Of course, the last one.

In the first case - the abundance of unnecessary words that only bore the listeners. In the second, all verbal garbage has been removed, but the semantic component is clearly lame: the sentence is dry, about anything. The third option is supplemented with the necessary details, which open to the listener a picture of what is happening. Living, "visual" phrases without parasitic words and unjustified repetitions are perceived and remembered much better.

If in 1987 President Ronald Reagan in his speech in front of the Brandenburg Gate in Berlin about the Berlin Wall said something like:

This wall is something umm ... that should not be there, so, in general, let's remove it as soon as possible.

Such a message would simply be lost in the information flow. Instead, a concise and capacious challenge was thrown:

Take down this wall!

The most frequent words are parasites: here, as if, simply, in general, this is the most, we will say, as they say, in short, like, I don't know, directly, it means so, yeah. If desired, it is not so difficult to get rid of these and other unnecessary "fillers". Here are three effective methods:

- Record your conversation on the recorder, and then listen and analyze. Evaluate whether it was possible to say something more briefly, whether you have words-parasites. Most likely, you will come to the conclusion that it is better not to fill in the pauses at all, than to insert muffled moans or extra repetitions into them.
- Ask a friend to record some annoying sound for you. This may be a loud beep or rattle. And may he turn it on every time you use the forbidden word in the conversation.
- Many people perceive information better in writing or in print. Try to make short notes (speeches, dialogues). Then reread them and ask yourself whether it is possible to make each sentence shorter, more imaginative and powerful. Of course, we all write and speak differently, each has its own style, but there are still general principles.

2. Problems with the rhythm of speech
Surely you noticed (if not for yourself, then for someone from the others) speech defects of a rhythmic nature. When words are pronounced abruptly, with too long pauses, or vice versa, the listener does not have time to understand his thoughts.

To experience a difference in perception, try saying the phrase below. Speak each syllable clearly and make short pauses between words. Listen to the sound of your speech:

Today I will go to the gym. Perhaps with a friend.

You will have the so-called "step" speech, in which too much emphasis is placed on the individual syllables, and this is a mistake.

And now try to mix each word with the next, so that you get one whole passage. Read without a hitch, but not too quickly:

Today-swim-gym-possible-girlfriend.

It may seem that this option sounds a bit careless. In fact, speech with such smooth transitions becomes easier for listening.

As for too fast pace, there is a risk not only to remain misunderstood, but also to blurt out something extra (for example, in a fit of emotions). Tracking the speed of speech will help, again, recording on the recorder.

Try to breathe in deeper before each sentence and think about what you are listening to with great interest and you have nowhere to hurry.

3. Failure to use body language
Many people know the difference between closed and open variants in body language, but continue to use closed gestures when they need to, on the contrary, open up.

Movement and facial expressions are characterized as open, if they express a friendly attitude and willingness to interact: when the palms are not hidden, the gaze is directed into the interlocutor's eyes, the feet are turned in his direction and the like. Closed gestures include crossed arms or legs, glancing to the side or at the phone, clenched fists - anything that shows tension or even aggression.

We all have natural inclinations to behave in one way or another, depending on the situation. If you do not agree with someone, the body automatically reacts: you narrow your pupils, turn your head, cross your arms. Conversely, when you are understood, listened and supported, you unknowingly open up.

However, it is not always necessary to give the interlocutor non-verbal signals, often the situation requires the opposite. Try to control your body movements and facial expressions when talking. Pay attention to the position of the arms, which muscles are tense. After practicing, you can manage it.

4. The habit of arguing
In itself, the expression of disagreement is not bad. As they say, truth is born in a dispute. So there are creative ideas, an incentive to learn and something to improve. All this is useful and necessary for social interaction, even if you are against many people.

Disagreement can be considered a mistake only when nothing depends on the consent or disagreement of the interlocutors and does not change. That is, if it is an empty dispute that does not bring any results, except for irritating opponents. The essence of such discussions is not to learn something new. When you claim that someone is wrong, you enter into a verbal battle for status with him. And that is why most of the debaters remain in their opinion - to preserve dignity.

The next time you hear a ridiculous or incorrect, in your opinion, point of view, first find out why the person thinks so, and do not rush to refute it.

If, even after listening to the arguments, you do not agree with someone's opinion, do not engage in a useless argument. Instead, transfer the conversation to another topic, where you can come to an understanding. There is no such area? Then just avoid communicating with this person.

5. Lack of topics for conversation
In an unfamiliar company or in a conversation with people who are new to you, words can quickly run out due to difficulties in choosing a common theme. Probably, each of us at least once in life had to pull out from himself some phrases, trying to fill awkward pauses. In order not to get into uncomfortable situations, you can come up with a list of on-call attendants in advance and use them on occasion.

Imagine the circumstances when you want to start a conversation with an unfamiliar or unfamiliar interlocutor: near the cooler at work, when you meet in a cafe, at a bus stop.

Prepare 10 topics that are suitable for talking with anyone in any situation.

It is easier than it seems. For example, you can always ask about life or work (of course, unobtrusively and delicately), discuss the latest news (but it is advisable to avoid politics), ask for advice on any issue. A win-win, albeit not very interesting option - conversations about the weather.

6. Illiterate speech
Do not forget that the conversation with a competent, educated person is perceived better than with those who are confused in cases and vocabulary accents. Increase your speech culture, read more, use dictionaries. But at the same time it is important to remember the sense of proportion: do not turn into a boring nerd and do not load the interlocutor with too complex phrases and terms.

9.2 DTR (Disrupt-Then-Refrain)
This technique is rather simple. Say something that seems to be out of context to offset your interlocutor. Within those words should have what you want. Then, make a statement that sounds pretty normal. Before your interlocutor can get

back on track to think about the "words behind a smoked screen", you must have made your message pretty clear, and he must have agreed with you already.

This is typically done in a single statement. You seemingly "disrupt", then you "refrain", and make a whole, unrelated point to get a positive response.

Conversely, this principle could also be used for a statement that you hear. If they are trying to say something, then break into it if you think it will not be to your benefit. Afterward, reply by giving a wrong meaning to the statement. This will get your interlocutor off balance and you will have tipped the scales in your favor.

The key here is breaking a set pattern, they hold on, you will get reframed statements that you will be able to work much better with.

9.3 Fear, anxiety and persuasion
All our fears, anxiety and complexes are programs designed to protect us from dangers. Only here the vast majority of fears are caused by social phobia. Not only do these fail to protect us from real dangers, but also stands in the way between us and a quiet life among people.

Judge for yourself, what is the real danger to our lives when we are going to approach to meet a girl? Or when are we going to stand up and make a toast in front of everyone? Or when we go on a first date? Naturally, there is no danger to life. So let's see what the cause of social fears is, and what the shortest way to get rid of them is. Only then will our power of influencing others be at its fore.

Social fears and anxieties are programs that are formed in a person as a result of certain psychological traumas in the past, which have undermined his self-confidence. For example, suppose there is a person who is afraid of public speaking. As an option, he could have formed this fear due to the fact that at school he was often laughed at when he went to answer the blackboard. As a result of this kind of injury, a person begins to "wind up" himself, savoring in his head various scenarios of what might happen the next time he has to speak to others.

What is the root of social fears that shapes them?
And then a person forms a series of flawed beliefs about himself and other people. For example, he can convince himself (on the basis of his own real negative experience) that he is a useless speaker and that people around are aggressively inclined and are just waiting for an opportunity to laugh at him and criticize him.

After that, his negative beliefs, influencing his thinking (making him pessimistic), undermine his self-esteem, creating the attitude that he is not able to speak publicly. Such is the pattern of the appearance of social fears. First, there is a series of psycho traumas (sometimes one will suffice if she left a strong impression of herself in a person), as a result of which a set of flawed beliefs are formed that make a person feel fear.

This process can be represented as a formula:

Desire + defective beliefs that question the attainability of the desired = fear.

For example, if you want to meet a girl in order to have a relationship with her (desired event) and at the same time you have flawed beliefs (for example, the conviction about yourself that you are an unattractive guy who cannot communicate with girls, plus the conviction about beautiful girls, that all they need is a boy-major, who will drive them through expensive restaurants and carry them in a limousine), then at the thought of meeting a girl you will have fear.

And such fear and anxiety will appear with you every time you think about coming up to meet the girl you like ... until you realize the inferiority of your beliefs and change them to more sound ones.

The most effective and fastest way to get rid of such fear (and other social fears) ... it is to work out the flawed beliefs on which your fear is based. As soon as you do this, you will no longer "go crazy" when you get into situations in which you have previously included fear.

Effective communication is one of the most important life skills that we can develop in ourselves, but many of us usually do not make enough effort to do this. If you want to become more sociable and better understand the people around you, here are some important tips that will help you to improve the effectiveness of communication.

1. Control your body language
You want to show your interlocutor that you are open for discussion, but at the same time your hands are crossed. You say that you are listening, but constantly cast your eyes on the phone screen.

Our non-verbal cues often show more than we think. No matter how well you can make eye contact or how you keep yourself in communication, do not forget that you constantly communicate, even when you do not say a word.

What are some ways to influence your body to communicate more effectively? Take an imperious pose if you need to increase your confidence before a serious conversation. Smile if you want to show your openness and friendly attitude. Learn to read other people's body language so that you can communicate in the best possible way.

2. Get rid of unnecessary words
"E" and "Um" do not do anything that can improve your speech or everyday communication. Exclude them from your vocabulary to be more persuasive and feel more confident. One of the ways to get rid of parasitic words is to start tracking when you say words like "This is the most" or "In short".

You can also take your hands out of your pockets or just relax and pause before you speak. A pause in a conversation will seem more awkward to you than to other people.

3. Planning a conversation
Conversation is an art that few people have mastered.

To fill in possible pauses in the communication process, especially when dealing with people you barely know, make a communication plan. The best topics to help eliminate awkward silence during a conversation should include everything related to family and leisure, occupation, as well as goals and dreams.

You will surely establish a common language with another person if you talk about what interests him.

4. Tell an interesting story
Stories have a huge impact. They activate our brain, make communication more intense, lively and interesting, and us - more convincing.

A told personal story can help with breaking barriers and influencing others.

5. Ask questions and clarify the words of the interlocutor
By asking questions and repeating the last few words of another person, you show interest in what he says, and also it will allow you to clarify points that may be misunderstood (for example, "Are you going to buy tickets for the Saturday match? Did I understand you correctly? ").

It also helps to develop a conversation and fill awkward pauses. Instead of trying to talk about the weather, ask questions (for example, "Are there any plans for the summer?" Or "What have you been reading lately?"). Be sure to discuss the answers, because it is more important to be interested than to seem interesting.

6. Eliminate distractions
It is rather unethical to dig into the phone when someone is talking to you.

You can not get rid of all the gadgets and technologies, but to postpone all these distracting things at the time of communication should not be a big deal for you.

7. Adjust to the listener.
The best speakers change their communication style depending on who they are talking to.

You probably would have used a different style of communication with colleagues or your boss compared to how you talk with your close friends, children or parents.

Always try to take into account the characteristics of another person when trying to convey information.

8. Be concise
For example, to correctly write a text message, use the following structure: "Background", "Reason", "Information", "Completion", "Conclusion (request, feedback)".

The information transmitted must be specific, consistent, complete and optimal, as well as ethical.

9. Put yourself in the place of the interlocutor
Communication is like a two-way street. If you have the opposite point of view, you can reduce the tension during the conversation, if you understand why the other person thinks otherwise.

For example, you should not prove anything to your interlocutor if he is too tired to carry on a conversation. The development of empathy (empathy) helps to better understand the process of communication, as well as improve the effectiveness of communication.

10. Listen and listen again.
The best thing you can do to develop your communication skills is learning how to listen to other people.

Focus your attention on the other person and let him speak without interrupting him. In fact, this is not so easy, but effective communication is a combination of spoken words that are intertwined with the ability to sincerely listen to another person. If you are not deprived of this quality, the other person is likely to listen to you as well.

Why is it so important to understand these points (1 - 10)? The ability to establish contact and develop relationships with other people has a strong positive effect on your whole life. It doesn't matter if you want to establish personal relationships or you want to increase the effectiveness of business communication, it is important for you to know how to become a great speaker, and listener. These are the first step to influencing others, as we humans are social creatures.

Communication skills are the key to building and developing friendships, creating a strong social support network. Communication skills help you achieve your goals with or without harming other people's values. People who do not have experience in effective communication do not know how to behave correctly in various situations in the process of communication. Some of us have the necessary skills, but they lack the confidence to use them. In any case, by practicing, you will increase your confidence and improve your communication skills.

Develop your confidence by interacting with other people. Develop communication skills that will enhance the ability to build successful relationships. Man is not born with the experience of effective communication. Like any other skill, it is practiced through trial and error, as well as repetition in practice.

9.3 Confidence

How to become sociable? Get confident.

Confidence in the process of communication is a sincere expression of one's own views, desires, and emotions, which inspires respect from the interlocutor. When you speak with confidence, your communication style is not condemned, and you are responsible for your own actions. If you depend on someone else's opinion, you may have difficulty expressing your thoughts and emotions openly.

Confidence skills can become difficult to master, especially if being confident to you means that you are not behaving as you normally would. You may be afraid of conflicts in the process of communication, always agree with the views of people around you, and also avoid expressing your own opinion. As a result of this behavior, you must have developed a passive communication style. Instead, you can seek to control and dominate others by developing confident communication skills.

A confident manner of communication carries many advantages. It will help you treat others more sincerely, reduce the level of anxiety and resentment. As a result, you get more control over your life and reduce the number of circumstances that do not depend on you.

Confidence is an acquired skill, not a personality trait with which you are born. Confidence is not part of your essence, because it arises as a result of performing the necessary actions, practices and disciplines.

Step 1. Identify problems
To begin with, ask yourself the following questions to determine which direction you should work in:

- Do I ask what I want?
- Is it difficult for me to express my opinion?
- How easily can I say "No"?

How to become confident in communication
Many people find it difficult to ask what they need, feeling that they have no right to ask or are afraid of the consequences of the question. You might think, "What if he says no?", Or "She thinks I'm rude and ill-mannered."

When you ask about something, it will be helpful to begin by expressing your understanding of the other person's problem. For example, "I know that you have been very busy lately." Then tell about the essence of your question and how you relate to it. For example, "This presentation should appear next Friday, and I am very worried that it will not be ready on time."

It is important to talk about your feelings, and not blame others. For example, it is better to say: "It hurts me when you are late for a meeting with me" than: "You are always late! You don't care about me! ". Then describe what you want from the other party. Be as brief and positive as possible. For example, "I would really like to understand how we can speed up the implementation of our project." Finally, tell the other party what he will receive in return if your request is granted. For example, "I would try to help create slides for the presentation next week."

Many people have problems with expressing their views openly. Perhaps you are waiting for others to express their opinion first, and only after that share yours if both opinions coincide. To be sure is to be ready to express your opinion, even if others do not, or your opinion is different from the views of other people. However, confidence means being able to accept new information and change your mind. However, this does not mean that you change your mind, because others think otherwise.

How to learn to say "No"
Saying "No" can be difficult if you are not confident enough. However, if you cannot say "No" to other people, you will not be able to take responsibility for your own life. When you say

"No", use the affirmative posture from the arsenal of non-verbal communication (stand up straight, look into your eyes, speak loudly).

Before you speak, decide what your position is.

If you find it difficult to say "No" right away, answer "I need time to think." This will help to break the vicious circle, when you always agree with the opinions of others. Remember, everyone has the right to say "No!".

Step 2. Develop your confidence.
First, make sense of the above when you avoid the opportunity to express your opinion, say "No" or ask what you need. How could you handle the situation differently?

Hone the skill of communicating out loud, being alone with yourself, so that you get used to the new way of having a conversation. For example, "Unfortunately, I can't help you this weekend," or "I want the work done before the end of tomorrow." Then simulate the situation that will arise next week, and in which you can show your confidence. Start by expressing your opinion or saying "No" to close people, and then use proven skills to communicate with other people. Rate how everything went. Pay attention to the reaction of the interlocutor. Could you do something different next time?

Remember that confidence is like any new skill and takes time and practice. Do not be too demanding to yourself at the very beginning, if you are worried, or do not understand how to do everything correctly. You will need time to get used to the new style of communication and the changes that will occur within you.

Although it is necessary to practice communication skills in practice, in order to better understand how to become sociable, you should carefully watch other people. Ask yourself, who do you feel comfortable communicating with? Study their behavior: smile, gestures, words, tone of voice.

Embed other people's chips in your life. Only then will you be able to embed yours in theirs.


9.4 How to persuade people to love you
You have only 90 seconds, so try to make a first impression of you perfect. Having achieved this, the opinion of you, most likely, will never change.
Fortunately, all people behave quite similarly - if you are enthusiastic and interested in them, they will most likely be enthusiastic and interested in you. But that is not all!


1. Use conversation
Show that you are genuinely interested and enthusiastic. Elementary, people love those who love them. If you can show sincere interest in the person you are talking to, and you will be enthusiastic about what he is saying, and even from meeting him in general, you will hit the target. You can then start saying any nonsense - they won't even notice.
How to do it? Smile, eye contact and focus attention on them. Ask questions. Engage. There are no complicated scientific theories here, all this is common sense (we will soon come to illogical moments). If you approach with a positive attitude, good intentions, you will succeed.


2. Ask questions
How else would you keep the conversation going? When you are involved with someone in a conversation, do not forget to ask questions about him. Most of the time, people like to talk about themselves, so it's pretty easy to like them if you listen well and take an interest in what they say. They themselves will not notice that they made up the bulk of the conversation! On the other hand, do not forget to bring in some interesting facts about yourself so that the conversation is two-sided. You need to ask open-ended questions (which cannot be answered simply yes or no), focus on the points that are common to you and show your personality. Therefore, instead of "I was also in London!" you had better say: "You were in London?

Incredible! I was there last spring with my tour group. What did you manage to see?".

3. Make compliments
The easiest and fastest way to get someone's sympathy almost instantly is to praise him. We all know that sometimes even the smallest compliment can set a good mood for the whole day. Just make sure that it is sincere! Saying "Uh ... I like the color of your teeth," you will not get a single fan. Praise them for their clothes ("Such a beautiful dress! It suits you very much.") Or for their actions ("Hmm, you tied up the laces cunningly, I need to try it too!"). It works efficiently, because it's natural, it's hard not to like someone who says nice things about you.

This tactic needs to be combined with other technique if you plan to be with this person for more than 90 seconds. Imagine that you have a friend who praises you once and for all. You would not believe a single word of his! Therefore, if you are planning long-term communication, use this move as an icing on the cake of your personality.

Find out their names. When you meet someone for the first time, it is expected that in the first of 90 seconds you will know their names - and then you have 89 more seconds for the rest of your magic. Remember them and use. At the end of the meeting, say goodbye and do not forget to name people by name, it will make the farewell more personal: "It was very pleasant to spend this evening with you, Anna, I hope we will see you again soon." Dale Carnegie said that the name of a person is the sweetest sound for him in all languages. So use it, then use it and use it.

5. Drain positive vibes
When engaged in a conversation, try to talk only about good or positive things. Hearing them is much more pleasant than something negative. Tell us how you like to do some hobby. Try not to say anything unpleasant, don't touch what you don't like - you only have 90 seconds to make a first impression and

you don't want the other person to decide that you have a pessimistic view of the world.

It is true, sadness and sympathy are a strong binding tool, but you should not use it in the first one and a half minutes of acquaintance. Leave this pearl of social tools until you get to know your interlocutors a little better. You need to become positive before making something negative.
For sure to remain positive, avoid self-admiration and boasting. Therefore, when the person with whom you are talking says "Aha, I just returned from London," you don't have to object to him "What, really? Yes, I've just come from Paris" and "Madrid!" This is not a competition. It is an honor for you to be in their presence, no need to make them feel the honor of communicating with you.

6. Speak their language. In the book "How to make people love you for 90 seconds or less", Nicholas Butman says that you need to "speak the language of your interlocutor." He argues this statement by the fact that according to the type of perception people are divided into visual, tactile and auditory modalities - having determined which type of perception is more important for a person, you can express yourself more clearly, more efficiently, and therefore more pleasant for the interlocutor.

It all sounds a bit abstract, right? The simplest example is to look at how the other person says "I understand." If he says "Yes, I see what you are talking about," most likely he is a visual. "Yes, yes, I hear you" - audial. And if he uses his hands - most likely kinesthetic.

7. Ask for a favor
Yes, you read everything right. This is known as the Benjamin Franklin effect - ask a person for a favor, and he will begin to love you more. You thought it was the opposite? You were very, very wrong. All this is due to the cognitive dissonance that comes to their mind. Who said it would be easy? The idea here is that if they do something for you (and they do, if you

ask for something insignificant), their subconscious will tell them: "Hmm ... I just did a favor to a person I almost I do not know ... Why did I do it? Oh, well, of course, I probably like him!" It sounds somewhat fragmentary until you realize that sometimes our behavior is determined by our thoughts - and this is just one of these moments.

8. Learn about what is happening in the world, how it works, and stand on your convictions.
Nobody likes people who just take up space and are no more fascinating than a wet blanket. Take time to explore the world in which you live - if not for yourself, then at least for more valuable conversations. You can make interesting comments that people will appreciate and thank you for, which will make you more interesting and memorable.

And if your point of view starts to criticize, stand by your convictions. If you start mumbling uncertainly and are not strong, you risk losing respect. People like those who are confident in themselves and in their views. So do not back down because of embarrassment! If you like Miley Cyrus - tell about it. If you hate puppies, well, just explain the reason and move on. Honesty is always the best policy.

9. Use body language
One - Smile
A smile makes you friendly, sociable and charming. If you didn't yet know, these three qualities attract most people! It turns out that no one likes to approach strangers and start a conversation themselves, so a smile is the first thing you can do to show that you are not afraid. Even the most confident people find it encouraging. And it's easy.

Two - Mirror them
It is about the following: adjust your posture and / or facial expression to them in such a way as if they are looking at their reflection in the mirror. On an unconscious level, this informs a person of your sympathy or approval of his feelings. Have you been to rock concerts that leave behind you this incredible

feeling - a single impulse, when you - one of a thousand of the same others - charge each other? This is due to all that you are doing in sync with the crowd - swinging, jumping, pushing. The same thing happens in a normal daily conversation! You need very few words (or not at all), and you still feel the connection.

If you do it purposefully 24 hours 7 days a week, you will most likely notice it. But for 90 seconds this trick will fit. So reflect the angle of their bodies, place your hands in the same position, and also, mirror their faces. You will probably also feel the exchange of energy.

Three - Maintain eye contact
Imagine a meeting with someone who is constantly looking a meter above your right shoulder. You literally have to force yourself to keep from waving your hand in the face of your interlocutor and not shouting, "Buddy! I'm here!". Deliver them from temptation and maintain good eye contact. This will show them that you are listening, interested and involved in what they tell you. Avoiding eye contact is often mistaken for rudeness.

If this is a problem for you, try to trick yourself by staring at the top of the other person's nose, or look at the person only at those moments when he speaks and rest from eye contact while you are speaking. You do not need to look at it 100% of the time. This will cause stress!

Four - Open body language
This is important in order to show your politeness and respectfulness - otherwise you risk appearing rude and unapproachable. In order to correctly present the picture, imagine a person with his legs crossed and his arms sitting in a corner, his eyes on the smartphone. Would you approach this person? Would you characterize it as "pleasant?" Probably not. Therefore, make yourself open and accessible, even if you think that no one is looking at you!

A sufficient amount of this - in addition to simply not crossing your arms and keeping your head up - just remain involved in what is happening around and be interested in the people who surround you. If your phone rings, ignore it. Show the person that you spend your time solely on him. Do not look at the clock, do not get distracted by the computer. Live this moment with the people around. The phone will stay with you, and people will leave.

Five - Use the power of touch
Suppose your colleague Michael says hello to you as you walk past your workplace. You will forget about it after 5 seconds. Now imagine that the same Michael, passing by your desk, casually shrugs your shoulder during the greeting. What will look more sincere? What more will arrange you to Michael? This is where the power of touch!

Now imagine what Michael says to you: "Hello, Sash, how did you get there? How was the weekend?" and touches your shoulder. He combined a touch, your name and a sincere, interested greeting. As it is now? Now we love our colleague Michael. Like very much.

Six - Make sure that your intonation, gestures and words match.
This is especially important when you are in a position of power or looking for a position of power - namely, at work. But it is also important when you try to convince people or simply express your point of view. If you want to inspire confidence and look sincere, all your manifestations must be consistent. Think of a lover who tells you "I love you" with clenched teeth and a clenched fist. "Wait, what?"

Most often this is noticeable by politicians. Loser politicians. You can often meet an elderly man who says, "I communicate with the younger generation. I know how they live," and at that time he shakes his fist, shows a finger or wrinkles his forehead. Nooo. It looks suspicious, and we feel it. This is a simple mistake that makes a significant difference.

10. Use your manners
One - Be confident
Weak personalities, one way or another, repel. Pompous people are unpleasant and repel even more obvious. But confidence attracts and attracts us, like moths on a flame. Therefore, in the 90 seconds that you have, hold your head high, put your shoulders back and smile. Exactly. You look cool, calm and collected. You know, now you are the one to whom people are drawn.
And if such a situation arises, press your hand firmly. A weak handshake turns most people away, especially in a professional situation. You need a handshake that would say: "I'm here! Yes, here it is me!". And not what would say: "I am here, I think, probably ... I am here?". Thank you but no.

Two - Dress accordingly
People judge by the first impression (this includes clothing), so make sure that you dress according to where you are going. Nobody likes a guy in home clothes in the middle of an expensive restaurant or a girl with baked makeup in the gym. Just as much as we don't like to admit it, clothing influences what we think about people - it's so simple, we can't resist and we can automatically draw conclusions. Therefore, whatever it is, dress according to the situation.
Do not forget to pay attention to details. Men can forget what the bright, brilliant watches say about them, and women - lose sight of the role of long, dangling feather earrings. Everything - starting with your shoes, make-up, hairdo and finishing with jewelry gives people around you a piece of information they collect about you. So pick up your equipment carefully, if you want to achieve the element of "love at first impression"!

Three - Adjust to their worldview
This is exactly the kind of "like stretching to like" you have heard of. Since people love those who seem to them to be like themselves, who have many similarities (especially in the first 90 seconds of the meeting), your chances of success will increase if you adapt to their worldview. Therefore, if they are

stiff and always do the right thing, or vice versa, they are a hippie and protest against the entire establishment — if you can easily understand their position, you can easily adapt to it. In other words, if there is a practical person in front of you, roll up your sleeves. If his tie is knotted like a hit, and the bottom of the shirt is knocked out of the pants - do not hesitate to take off your shoes. If they have a big Latte from Starbucks in their hands - answer them with anti-capitalist remarks. Use all those visual hints that you can, and embody them in your own way, in your style.

Four - Do not be afraid to get ridiculed
Jennifer Lawrence was incomparable in the "Hunger Games", and then fell down the stairs, receiving that award, and became even more matchless. Therefore, when you overturn a latte on yourself, under new jokes of new friends - relax. In fact, it can play in your favor if you do not scare yourself. They will think about it just as much as you will, so long live these spots! They emphasize the brown tint of your eyes, I guess.

Everyone is pleased to understand that they are dealing with real people. Inside we are all stupid seventh graders, afraid to get caught in the nose. Take yourself (and make fun of it), show that you are real (and still cool). Well, what a relief!

Tips
- In the conversation, talk about common things that do not imply a tough personal position. This is because if you start talking about something controversial, you run the risk that the opinion of the other will be very different from yours, and the result will be a collision. After that you will need more than 90 seconds to get that person to love you again.
- If you have a bad day, stay at home. It is difficult to get rid of a bad mood, and people mistakenly take it for negativism. Wait until your mood improves if you want others to love you!
- When you maintain eye contact, you don't need to stare at them like an eccentric. Just look into their eyes when

they say something important, or at least important to them.


9.5 Persuasion and sentimental relationships
To persuade a person or persons with whom you are in a sentimental relationship, you must be confident and full of confidence. As a first step, you must understand the kind of relationship you have and agree to ask yourself a few questions about yourself. In a second step, you must make sure that your interlocutor ex has also evolved to be on rational terms with you.

During your first new communication you must be positive, dynamic, and take things lightly. From the first contact, you must let a certain amount of mystery hover over you. your interlocutor probably thinks he knows all about you and that you do not book any surprises, make him understand that he is wrong! Your first exchanges must serve to establish a new communication, without proposing an appointment or asking anything, you just have to communicate.

Once you have renewed communication, you will gradually create your place. Indeed, once the communication is resettled, that it is almost fluid (or almost), then it came time for the meeting. It is important to keep the communication, even in case of refusal. Then maintain the exchanges and reiterate, when you will feel more affinities ....

Finally, we must accept that communication will not always go in your direction, and that's normal. Anyway, always be positive, do not be influenced by the negative but on the contrary, influence others positively. Know that this is as much to win back this fellow(s), so never give up.

Conclusion

Persuasion is an essential element of almost any interaction. This applies to all types of relationships. Persuasion is the impact on the interlocutor to change his attitude towards something, if he holds a different opinion. To influence a person, it is important that a change in attitude also changes a person's actions.

The perfection of the persuasive effect is manifested in the fact that a person does not so much do what he is recommended, how much he wants to do it. From this it follows that the goal of persuasion is to transform your own desire "I want you ..." to the desire of the persuaded to do it - "I also think so now because...". However, in order for the interlocutor to want to do what you want, you must first reach an understanding with him, without which it would be impossible to incline him to his point of view.

The most important forms of understanding are the following: recognition, identification of the cause, determination of the consequences.

Recognition is perhaps the simplest form of understanding, and it consists in the ability to relate a subject, phenomenon, or attitude to a group or category.

Identifying the cause is already a somewhat more complex manifestation of understanding, since here, in relation to the sphere of relationships between people, a more complex skill is needed - identifying the motives of people's behavior, that is, what motivates them to act.

The definition of a causal relationship between phenomena or processes predetermines the well-known principle of determinism. Its practical essence lies in the fact that, having understood the principle (the above form of manifestation of understanding), we are less inclined to reject the consequence. On the other hand, the essence of determinism boils down to the following: the knowledge of the action (effect) depends on the knowledge of the cause.

I hope you liked my book. Do not forget, some of these steps take time and some practice. Afterward, I am very sure that you will be able to influence any and everyone that you wish to when you have fully mastered these techniques.

Book Description

In the book "Influence Human Behavior" Inijah says that anyone can learn the skills of persuasion. He tells how to do it.

In a modern information society, interpersonal communication and the information we receive is very important. After all, all this affects us, our ideas and dreams. The impact is not only through personal communication, but also through advertising, television, radio, the Internet. You can also highlight the impact of people on each other, the impact of a person on a group or the influence of a group on a person.

To most people, the ability to influence others seems fantastic. Some people easily manage to convince others of the loyalty of their ideas. Others are constantly forced to go on about. The author of the book believes that everyone can learn the skills of persuasion. In his book, he made available, without undue scientific knowledge, the information known to him. The narration is conducted in some places with humor that will not let you get bored, examples from the experience of the writer and his friends are given. The book offers interesting tests and facts from all around the globe.

The author does not propose to use the skills of persuasion to the detriment, for cruel manipulation of people. He is humane to this issue. For many people, this information both prove useful for the purpose of controlling other people, as for understanding when someone is trying to influence them. Understanding when advertising affects you, the crowd, even family members in the aggregate, you can save yourself from committing actions that do not correspond to true desires. After all, how many cases are known when a person listened to someone, and then regretted his action. Knowing how persuasion techniques look like, their use in appropriate cases will help many to improve relationships with colleagues, boss, with family and friends. Therefore, this book will be useful to any reader.